Martin Newell
SELECTED POEMS

To Leanne

love

Martin
the
Newell

Martin Newell
SELECTED POEMS

Foreword by
Germaine Greer

Jardine Press Ltd
2008

Also by Martin Newell

I Hank Marvinned
Under Milk Float
The Illegible Bachelor
Poetic Licence
New! Top Poetry
This Little Ziggy
Wildman of Wivenhoe
Black Shuck
The Song of the Waterlily
Late Autumn Sunlight
A Return To Flanders
Spoke'n'Word
A Prospect of Wivenhoe

www.martinnewell.co.uk

First published in 2008
by Jardine Press Ltd
20 St John's Road,
Wivenhoe, Essex CO7 9DR
www.jardinepress.co.uk

Printed by Printwright
6 Boss Hall Business Park,
Ipswich, Suffolk IP1 5BN

ISBN 978-0-9552035-6-5

Contents

ACKNOWLEDGEMENTS

I should like to give acknowledgements and thanks for this volume and permission to reprint the work herein:

To Dr Joe Allard of the Literature Department of the University of Essex.

To *The Independent* and the *Independent on Sunday*, for whom I wrote between 1990 and 2005.

I should like to give special thanks to *The Sunday Express* for their permission to reproduce work here.

I should like to thank James and Catherine Dodds and the staff at Jardine Press, who continue to publish and present my work in its very best light and to Professor Germaine Greer for her kind foreword to this volume. I'd like to acknowledge and thank the Wivenhoe Bookshop for their support over the years and finally Charlotte Bernays and John Cooper Clarke for lending an ear to my work when it was in progress.

FOREWORD

by Germaine Greer

It's a good thing that way back in the seventies or eighties Martin Newell didn't ask me to take a look at his poetry and tell him what I thought. I'd probably have told him what I usually tell would-be poets, that he should read more poetry than he wrote, and that poetry is not just letting it all dribble down the page. Not that I think it would have been the end of him, because it's clear you couldn't stop him writing if you sawed his hands off. He's said it himself, that he wasn't interested in getting things perfect. Nor should he be. A haiku may be perfect but Newell has no ambition to become a paragon of imperial courtly culture. Even Pound pretty quickly lost interest in poetry as netsuke.

Rough and ready gives you impact and effect rather than perfection. Spontaneity is the only way of generating the energy that has to drive non-lapidary writing. If Newell had pussyfooted round with sonnets and villanelles, squeezing his perceptions into elegant shapes rather than plunging headlong into a stream of associations, you wouldn't get the perfect bits that pop up like water-voles. 'Lime-green Easter afternoon', for example, is a little gem spun off by the whirring stream of consciousness that comes from the brain of a cycling man. There it is – the whole mashed-lettuce experience of early spring in the east of England – in three words.

Most spinners of quotidian rhymes spin them in tetrameters. This is a tradition as old as balladry itself; the result is usually contemned by the purveyors of regulation pentameters as doggerel. In common with all our vernacular poets Newell is imbued with the metre of the hymns he sang as a schoolboy. What was good enough for Blake is good enough for him. At the risk of exposing myself as a pompous old lady don, I'd like to point out that there is a five-line tetrameter stanza in Newell's armamentarium that's a bit special.

Let's bomb across a bombsite
On bikes that have no gears
Where brakes are just for cissies
And tumbles hold no fears
On cross bars of the years

You could read this as two longer lines, followed by a shorter one; if there were three of the longer ones you'd have something like a Sapphic stanza. As it is, this is about as close as you can come to the Aeolian form without crashing. Newell would grin at the thought that he is being compared to the hairy-legged foundress of lyric verse, but I'll bet he has as much in common with her as he has with Wordsworth.

Inasmuch as it was Wordsworth who first advised poets to use the ordinary language of men (not gentlemen) rather than a specific poetic diction, Newell is his heir, but he is closer in sensibility to Clare – not the Clare who spoiled his most vivid insights by embalming them in the frigid diction of Thomson and his ilk, but the Clare who wrote his best, as Newell does, in blunt tetrameters. When Clare was unintimidated by better educated poets, he produced a vivid unpunctuated present-tense narrative of what he was seeing and hearing, as Newell tends to do. What both poets see and hear, of course, is governed by their sensibility. Not everybody would compare dew-drops to fishes' eyes as Clare does. Not everybody notices that an aged cat is 'ridged of spine' or that the railway tracks of Essex are edged with rosebay willow herb and ragwort or that summer rain makes 'penny-blots', as Newell does.

Though Newell says himself that there aren't enough odd words in these poems to justify a glossary, and certainly he isn't a dialect poet, I can't deny a strong desire to write a po-faced companion to the works of Martin Newell, explaining the echoes and references that throng on every page, here a bit of Masefield, there Bob Dylan or Dylan Thomas, a nod to Auden, even Yeats. Newell might believe that it is enough to be relevant to the 'now' but he is as sensitive as any poet must be to the fact that the 'now' is well on the way to being the 'then' even before he has begun to write about it. There is both a historic and an elegiac dimension to his work. If 'contemporary' is not to mean 'temporary', the rich world of demotic culture that Newell evokes mustn't disappear from memory with its catchwords. Supposing a variorum edition is one day planned, it would be the best fun in the world to put together a dyspeptic Johnsonian commentary explaining what 'Jeyes' is or Vanguard shoes, or a Briggs & Stratton, or how it might be that dinner ladies might come to work in a Saracen and what kind of a cruel and stupid thing an Asbo is. Explaining Newell's 'buildings plonked like Toblerone' would occasion a rancorous description of the expansion of poorly designed 'low-cost' housing in the Thames Gateway and beyond, low-cost to the builder that is, not to the buyer, as well as something about mass-produced Swiss chocolate. Even more rewarding would be the chance to explicate and illustrate the mind-numbing humbuggery that provokes a jeu d'esprit like 'The Winterval Manifesto'.

People who don't much like poetry will like these poems, but poetry-lovers should enjoy them too. More important than the placing of them on library shelves would be the keeping of them in your bicycle basket, to read when you're munching your cut-lunch among the cow parsley, or in the pocket of your anorak, to take a look at while your dog is investigating something under a hedgerow. The endpapers should be the map of Essex. Some will say there are surprisingly few love poems, and those oddly indirect. The whole volume is a love poem, to Essex, the least gentrified, most countrified and most idiosyncratic county in Britain. No other county could have produced a Martin Newell, descended as he is on both sides from Essex man.

> Man of Essex, thoroughbred
> Lead in pencil, gear in shed,
> Brass in pocket, books in red,
> Always kept his ferrets fed.

WIT AND WHIMSY

I WANNA BE A GOTH

I wanna be a goth
I wanna be a goth
I wanna wrap myself
In a long black cloth
Sit around a cemetery
Worship Thoth
I'm happy being serious
I wanna be a goth

I wanna form a band
It's gotta be the same
As every other band
With a German name
Pile on the doom
Sing about the pain
Only every smile
If it pours with rain

I wanna meet a girl
She's gotta wear lace
With dyed-black hair
And a long thin face
Big black eyes
On a lead-white base
And make goth love
In a nice dark place

I wanna be a goth
I wanna be a goth
With all the joie-de-vivre
Of a three-toed sloth

Blackness attracts me
Unlike a moth
I go towards the darkness
I wanna be a goth.

BEOWULF'S RETURN TO THE ESTUARY

So the Hwyfe and I and our three scyldren
took the hring hroad. Which was a mistaek
Bumper-to-bumper through the Dartfeord Tunnel
Fynally eonding up neare Grays. An healfing nightmaer!
The scyldren at each otheres hthroates and the Hwyfe
bewailing the loss of her Hrattner's gold signum
given to her by Hrothgar, eofter the Great Feast
hwen he hyospitalised her brothere Hwayne.

On the hway back to Gyllingham, we stopped in
at a Harvestyr – which was packed and then
into a Mead Hall eofter I dropped off Hwyfe and scyldren.
Three flasks in and a mighty battle started. This was
because of some warriors just off a longship at Chatham.
One of these was well eout-of-ordur, adorned with gold
tatooed around the neck and sheouting the odds.

I mean, there was only me, Hygelac the Bald and Welnaf.
Welnaf, fearsome in his scyell-suit, is a bit naughty in a hruc
and says to this doughnut: "Oi gaezer! Are you calling me
a Cnut?" That hwas it. The hwole thing went pear-scyaped.
Then came this Grendel. Took a Styanley knife to Hygelac
and gleassed Welnaf in the fyace. In absence of a shootyr,
I took a poolcyu to the beorstard and he hwent down.

Back at Hrothgar's Hall, Hrothgar said: "That won't be the
eond of it, you mark my words." Scyure enuf, two
days latere, I'm leaveing the Mead Hall when Daerren says:
"Oi, Beowulf, there is a grate fyre in the Carpeork!"
I looked and the Grendel had torched my Feord Escyort.

Eofter that, I leoft it. Since Welnaf's brothere's put the hword
eout that He hwill deal hwith the Grendel. But quietly.
And the Hwyfe doesn't want my two hyears suspended
being brought up agaen. So that hwas that.

DEAD IN THE BARMAID'S BED

Plywood coffin draped in sacks
Funeral feast of crisps and snacks
Poor man's Prozac – Special Brew
Massive turn-out, guests all knew
This is what the vicar said:
"Found him dead in the barmaid's bed."

Found him dead in the barmaid's bed
Lacy knickers on his head
What with all the gossip spread
Bound to raise his local cred.

Women tutted, men said, "Odd
There but for the grace of God
Not behaviour I'd endorse..."
Envious as hell of course
Seeing him in that state of grace
Hard to keep a serious face

Should have legged it. Died instead
Found him dead in the barmaid's bed.

Man of Essex, thoroughbred
Lead in pencil, gear in shed,
Brass in pocket, books in red,
Always kept his ferrets fed.
Found him dead in the barmaid's bed
Found him dead in the barmaid's bed
"Good owld buoy" they quietly said.
Found him dead in the barmaid's bed.

HEROIN IN WHISKAS

There's heroin in Whiskas
I'm reasonably sure
The cat's getting desperate
Pacing the floor
He hangs round the food cupboard
Waiting to score
Wild-eyed and reckless
Quick on the claw
He's sharing a needle
The cat from next door
Comes round at mealtimes
And ties-off his paw
They shoot up together
And beg me for more
Who should I turn to?
The vet – or the law?

There's heroin in Whiskas
I don't *think* it's crack
He said he could handle it
Lying on his back
But last night the chemist's
Came under attack
The only things missing
Were chocolate and smack
And some halibut oil
From the vitamin rack
He won't have the dried stuff
Which comes in a pack
If it ain't got the tincture
He reckons it's cack.

There's heroin in Whiskas
And reasonably pure
He completely refuses
To go for a cure
He just lies around
Till it's time for his feed
But what makes it worse –
Is the dog's taking speed.

MISS L HOLDEN

Supposing...
I married the girl
In the building society
Miss L Holden
Lynn, I later found out
With her CFC hair

And her strong leanings
Towards normality
With her grey suit
And her ruffy blouse
Not *too* high heels
Supposing I just woke up
And found myself married to her?
Could I bring myself to like
Her Lionel Richie cassettes?
Her Jackie Collins books?
Her Daily Mail feminism?
Her: "Mrs-Thatcher-may-be
A-complete-psychopath
But-she-says-what-she-*thinks*."
How would I cope with
Going to Florida
For two weeks sunbathing?
What would I do
while all
Those soap operas were on TV?
What about sex?
I expect I'd have to
Take a shower first
And ultimately
There might be a baby
Then I'd be forced
To go to the christening
And talk with the women
About job prospects
With the men
About cars and football
The answer might be
A computer course
Then while Lynn was at home

Nursing little Lionel
I could be on the 6.15 am
From Colchester to Liverpool Street
In my Burton raincoat
And my Hepworth suit
Going to work in computers
Somewhere in London
And *dreaming*
Of doing the square lawn
Of our Barratt Home.
With a Flymo
On Sundays
There would be a lunchtime pint
Or driving in the car
To her mum's
I would sensibly
Not be under-insured
Go to the freezer centre
Take up D I Y
Be adventurous in bed
By getting some books
On the subject
Pay Lynn little compliments
About her hair
Still give her Valentine cards
Great big ones
With a giant, shiny, rayon heart
And a pre-written message
Build a shelf
For baby things
While she read a catalogue
Yes I think perhaps
I could be quite convincing
But what would happen

If I cracked?
Supposing she came home one day
And found me completely naked
In the garden
Except for a Napoleon hat?
Being wheeled round and round
On a small trolley
Pulled by two sheep
And shouting with laughter?
Or what would happen
If I turned the spare bedroom
Into The Temple of Ra
Painted symbols on the walls
Burned incense
And took strong hallucinogens
Chanted mantras late on Thursday nights
And had spiritual experiences?
How would she cope
With monthly Sufi meetings
Or rebirthing
In a big tank
In our living room?
Supposing I lent the garden shed
To a French-Vietnamese lesbian
Who needed to finish her novel?
Would Lynn mind?
I think she would
Her parents
Mr and Mrs Holden
Most certainly would
They would be onto their solicitor
Like a shot
Finding out what could be done
Police and psychiatrists might come

Lynn would be tearful
But determined now
I'd lose my job
The two sheep and myself
The French-Vietnamese lesbian novelist
We'd all be homeless
And even though
I never married
Miss L Holden
From the building society
I can't forgive her for that.

ROUND THE COUNTIES

You Worcestershire my Bedfordshire?
You only broke my Hertfordshire
In shanga-langa Lancashire
And la-de-da-de-Derbyshire
A simple breach of Essex here
A flash of pubic Herefordshire
You grabbed me by the Hampshire
Now I'm stuck in missing Lincolnshire
I'm sorry that I Cambridgeshire
Took Cleveland all my senses there
But nothing succeeds like Sussex
I'm so Surrey

I'd come whenever you Cornwall
I must be such a Kent
I've Durham all to death
But the chance was Devon-sent
I bop shoo-wop Shropshire
Spent three days in de-tOxfordshire
I had a sense of Gloucestershire
But you couldn't care Leicestershire
You told me you would Suffolk-ate
But Warwick you expect from me?
You tied me up in Notts.

You shouldn't pass the Buckinghamshire
You just can't get the Staffordshire
Your bite's worse than you Berkshire
It's not a game of Cheshire
You wouldn't igNorthumbria
Have Merseyside upon me
Cos I think I'm going to Cumbria
Not forgiven Norfolk gotten
Sorry if the ending's rotten
I couldn't in Dorset
But how should you be Avon
Occasions like this?
My place or Yorks?
Thanks
But Northants.

A HOUSE IN FRANCE

House in France, A House in France
I'm going to buy a House in France
I'll write my magnum opus there
I'm bound to get the book advance.

House in France, House in France
My friends have got them – why not me?
I'll say that I "divide my time"
Looks brilliant on the old CV:
Ah yes, well he divides his time
Between his Essex home and France
The food, the wine, the pace of life
The French know how to live, all right
We'll spread ourselves across Provence
And have our friends round every night.

Here, guess how much my house is worth?
The one I bought in *France*, my dear
Combien le prix de ma maison?
I've heard they're shooting up round here
The French of course, they think we're mad
Buying run-down gites with dodgy bogs
But still, we've found this little man
Who fixes roofs and chops the logs
And everybody's moving now
The whole of England's middle class
Reversing in their four-wheel drives
To cram up France's dusty arse.

And when I get my house in France
Divide my time twixt here and there
Ardeche, Provence or Aquitaine

I'll lay my wounded spirit bare
Paint poxy pictures, sit and write
Some dreadful Booker masterpiece
And only come to England
When my tenants need a rent increase.

House in France. House in France
Witter, witter, House in France
We've fucked up England with our greed
It's time to give the French a chance.

Alors, et comment allez vous?
The girls are all like Betty Blue
The men are Gerard Depardieu
Avez vous une cloppe? Bien sure!
La verisimilitude a confiture
Je boire la pisse du vache
A cherie bi-bi co-co lo
Excusez moi, mais je dois crache!

House in France, House in France
Wibble wibble, House in France
The only trouble with The French;
You shout at them, they look askance.

House in France, House in France
Somewhere in the *south* of France
Near Montpellier or Toulon
Where's my Bierritz crash-course gone?
Perhaps you'll *rent* my House in France?
Waffle waffle, House in France
J'attempt apprender votre langue
It's been a right old song and dance.

House in France House in France
Neurotic whining, middle class
Pretentious, artsy English twats
In sandals, socks and floppy hats
Moaning in their dizzy herds
While drunken hunters shotgun birds
Or take out cyclists, cows and sheep
Before they have their lunch and sleep.

House in France House, in France
Oh, you've bought one? Really? When?
Good. Leaves Essex free for me.
Best of luck. Well... Piss off then.

CURSORY RHYMES

Humpty Dumpty stood by a wall
Safely stopped from risking a fall
Signs were up in several places
Banning all embryo/wall interfaces.

Little Ms Muffet sat on a tuffet
Eating her 5-a-day.
Along came a spider
On cocaine and cider
And heisted her laptop away.

The Grand Old Duke of Talk
He had ten thousand chaps
He marched them off to the Middle East
Cos he thought he should, perhaps
And once they were there, it was bad

But after a while it was worse
It was sad, insane and an awful drain
On the dwindling public purse.

There was a young woman
Who lived in a shoe
With prices so high
It was all she could do.

As I was lying on the stair
I phoned a man who wasn't there
He wasn't there again today
Carer job-shares get that way.

MY SELF-EMPLOYED OFFICE PARTY

Went self-employed in 'Ninety-one
It has its pitfalls, lack of fun
And overwork had left me tired
Some sort of party was required
As boss *and* workforce talking here
I'm not as hard as I appear
Though disagreements *had* occurred
And when they did, I had a word
About myself, and *with* myself
Though mainly, seemed to like myself
Till halfway down that jug of port
I told myself just what I thought.

The problems with the new IT
Were mainly what defeated me
The thing I found the most frustrating?

Constant crises, with updating
As boss *I* sympathised with this
But what about a Christmas kiss
Perhaps under the mistletoe?
I told myself I ought to go
But drinks went down, the discs went on
The Kylie, ABBA, Elton John.
I'd warned myself about this stuff
I didn't listen hard enough.

Well, that's the last thing I remember
This occurred in mid-December
To the week, a year ago
And this tribunal ought to know
As sole employer/employee
I've always liked a laugh with me.
But fondle my *own* buttocks? Ah!
I definitely went too far.
Look... it was just a bit of fun.
A boss and worker one-to-one
Though *I've* proved harder to convince
And haven't spoken to me since.

The outfit which I wore that night?
Provocative! Well, rather tight.
I cried and grabbed my coat to go.
I've *got* to learn that No means *No.*
I stopped the party, locked the place
And now there's this harassment case.
What can I say? *I'm* in the wrong.
Though, having known myself so long
I'd always thought I was a friend
It's awful that it's had to end
In dragging myself off to court.
This year. I'm staying away from port.

THE QUEEN'S OWN YOBS

The Queen's Own Yobs
The 'Quoys' for short
Recruited from a British street
Were hand-picked by a Brigadier
Who trained them as a new elite
With unlaced trainers on their feet
Each new recruit made his salute
With middle-finger. Discipline
Was tight. The sergeant bawled
"Oright?"
The yobs rejoindered
"Wick-ed. Skin!"
The first crack unit
that there'd been,
To be on crack to guard the Queen
Not only did it help them fight
It kept them all awake at night.

On duty in the combat zone
A Queens Own Yob
Could last a year,
On barely more than chewing gum,
A bag of chips and cans of beer.
The enemy might wake at dawn
His ammunition store unlocked
His radio missing and in pawn
And all his tanks and jeeps
been twocced.
Late on parade, the Brigadier
Said, "Very good indeed, so far"
You've done me proud, lads
Just one thing,
Has anybody seen my car?"

THE WINTERVAL MANIFESTO

Shepherds watching flocks by night
Must cease work by 9.00 pm
In line with set working hours limits.

The cattle are lowing?
The baby awakes?
Ring our Noise Pollution Hotline.

The holly and the ivy
Now they are both well known
Have been deemed unsuitable for use
Since the holly is not child-friendly
And the ivy may affect asthma-sufferers.

Boxing Day is re-scheduled for January 2nd.
Re-named *Courtesy Visit/ Gift Interface Day*
This will allow workers in non-aligned jobs
A compensatory Comfort and Joy interlude.

Differently-nosed sub-arctic deer
Must not be subjected to workplace harassment.
And will receive fair employment assessment
Under the Equal Opportunities Act.

Safety headgear must be worn at all times
In a one-horse open snow vehicle
Laughing all the way.

Our Winterval Patriarch will visit you
He may seek to gain entry via your chimney
We apologise if he calls at an inconvenient hour
Under the 1994 Toy Recipients' Charter
You may be entitled to compensation.

THE FOURTH FORM AT ST ASBO'S

The 4th form at St Asbo's School
Whose uniform was black and blue
Wore hoods on caps which as a rule
Would indicate their high IQ
The teaching staff, with much to do
Resided in a garrison
Except the dinner ladies who
Came in each day by Saracen.

A sniper watched the entrances
Informing pupils who were late
And parents come to remonstrate
To leave their weapons by the gate
The dads not serving sentences
On average, they were twenty-eight
Were in this way brought up to speed
Since many of them couldn't read.

St Asbo's 4th form's leading lights
Were mumbling, disadvantaged mites
Yet when arrested, on most nights
Recited clearly all their rights
And demonstrated to a man
– Despite a short attention span
A strong reluctance to forgive
And motto: "We know where you live."

St Asbo's head – an ex-marine
Though educationally green
Had worked in Basra and Belize
Could face down riots and RPGs
And easily secured the job

By cracking down on every yob
With punishments to fit the crime:
And skiing trips at Easter time.

The 4th form at St Asbo's ways
Earned every single child straight A's
As well as merit-marks and stars
Plus stolen I-pods, phones and cars
Inspectors looked approving on
With bad old-fashioned teaching gone.
What better start could youngsters need?
The best days of their lives indeed.

THE VICAR RECRUITMENT RAP

C of E
It's the one for me
We're talking Three (feat Trini T)
Your mobile soul-phone
Comes for free
It's a Friends & Family to
Big G

Gimme a V now gimme an I
Add a C A R to the other side
Heaven's gate is a Park'n'Ride
Who d'ya call
When your granny's died?
Vicar
Say that name with pride

Service time and the bells go *clang*
It's a happenin' clappenin' kinda thang
From a warm-up prayer in the vestibule
To a chilled out church
And an ambient Yule
Tho' the Sno B deep
The wind B Krool
The smell of Faith is a cool Kagoul

V is for Vespers
I 4 an eye
The sermon's hot
But the ink ain't dry
For those in peril on the C
You who would A pilgrim B
No R&R on the Sabbath day
Can the dude deliver?
Yes, way

More E, Vicar?
Not 4 me
X-cept E-clesiastically
When the work comes in
Gotta make that call.
Yo! Corinthians
Quit it.
Paul.
(pp Father, Son and Ghost)
The Devil's illin'
But he's toast.

YOUR POST OFFICE

You cannot quantify a thing
That's best-defined by stamps and string
And such statistics in your hands
Mean nothing next to rubber bands

The civil servant in his seat
Evaluating loss of heat
When doors are opened to the street
Won't know, that it is where you meet

The 'old days' are all good and well
If somewhat of a bagatelle
Efficiencies though, must be made
In sherbet dabs and lemonade

Such niceties go in the bin
When auditors poke noses in
Along with Victory Vs and pegs
Binbags, candles, free-range eggs

And all this friendly village chat
– Even the shop's adopted cat –
Won't help pensioners begin
Grappling with their chip and PIN

Take comfort from computers, cars
And family-oriented bars
So when we shut your branches down
You won't feel any less a town

We understand of course we do
In terms of pencils, pads and glue

In chapels though, where money sings
We do not care about such things.

MA AND PA SALUTE KING CAR

Ma and Pa salute King Car
The dirty despot roars and squeals
Yummy Mummy thinks it's scrummy
When her wendy-house on wheels
Whizzes through Edwardian crescents
Past the card-less, car-less peasants
Hacking down Crimea Street
Queenie in her comfy seat
Bike-rack, bullbars, dog beside her
Sat-nav Prozac voice to guide her
Tells us why and who we are
Ma and Pa salute King Car.

Bad King Car, the filthy bastard
Far too greedy. Thanks to him
Fat despairing twenty-somethings
Have to drive – to reach the gym
Bubble-headed, weeble-wobbles
Used to think that Central Locking
Was a village in the Midlands
Where they first invented twoccing
Children's school in bandit country?
Over miles of rock-strewn tundra
Is it, lady – Is it really?
– That the myth you labour under?
Four wheels favours fatter arses
Tescos deep in mountain passes

Buggered if they'll walk so far
Ma and Pa salute King Car.

"Well... I don't like cars much either
But I have to have one – yaah?"
Had a transport seminar
Which is why I bought my car
Almost two whole miles from here
Travel exes all completed.
Couldn't walk. Suppose it sleeted?
– And the bus would be too dear.
Nope. Fat car's the only answer
Big fat four-wheel munter, Boy
Me puffed up in Puffa jacket
Howling at the hoi-polloi.
Politicians couldn't hack it
Far too loaded for the voters
Oh they'll hammer drinkers, smokers
Over-eaters, then they'll focus
On the health and welfare issues
Blow into the same old tissues
What they won't touch is the driver
Do we have a Cycling Czar?
Course not. We won't get one either.
Ma and Pa salute King Car.

Soon we'll make a future car
The eco-lesion, suture car
One speed, two-shade, mobile shed
Yellow polka dots on red
Top speed – forty miles an hour
Chicken-shit and solar power
Need a motor? There's just one.
But no status and no fun.

Nothing there to make you proud
And the only car allowed
There's no butchness and no buzz
Gets you there, that's all it does.
Car to suit our fragile times
Fitted out with ice-cream chimes
That should make the boys feel silly
It's the car that's not a willy
And it plays a stupid tune
Be afraid. It's coming soon.

In the meantime, Superstar
Ride that roadway, tame that tar
Whack that track to hell and back
Cancer, stroke and heart-attack
Kill that walker. Maim that dyke
Knock that hippie off his bike
Pig that pavement, hog that street
Petrolhead on techno-beat
Parliament will keep you sweet
'Less he wants to risk his seat
Road Rage – V(ery) C(ross) and Bar
Ma and Pa salute King Car.

DO YOU TAKE THIS MAN

– upon gay marriage

Do you take this man to be
Your lawful wedded chap and bloke
To pool your records and your books
To designate who cleans, who cooks
Unblocks the drains, puts shelving up
While burnishing the loving cup?

Do you take this geezer/guy
To face the slings, as time slips by
Of taut parental prejudice
While striking out for wedded bliss
Till Mum comes round to visit you
Then, after several years, Dad too?

Do you take this mush, this John
To split the usual carry-on
De-flea the cat, hose down the dog
Or bend a ballcock in the bog
Rake out the cinders, set the fire
And then de-fluff the tumble drier?
Since after kisses, cakes and rings
Marriage is about such things.

The group of friend who'll pack the room
For bride and bride, or groom and groom
Bring toasters, kettles, cruet-sets
The same as they might do for hets
Who keen and strain and yearn to be
Handcuffed through all eternity.

So if you take this man, this dude
Whatever moral good accrued
Through love, commitment, piety
As statement to society
They'll understand it well enough
It's marriage, Chief. It's normal stuff.

SIR GAWAYNE AND THE GRENE KNIGHT

The kynge's crewe chilled at Camelot that Christemass
With many tasty geezeres gotte up in good geare
Blokes with a reppe, well-rayted in a rukke
People who culde partie with a vengeance
The do went onne for dayes and dayes
Arthur's burde mucked-out the place some mornynges
Emptied ashetrays, clered out caque and cannes
Hoovered-up the roachez and the rubyshe
Come middaye, it all went raydeo rentals agayne
For they were as a Millwalle posse, bygge-style
All of themme on St Ella biere and shortes
                    all daye.

> Laddes drunke and stinking
> Loades of booze and scoffe
> Everybodye thinkeing
> Somethynge myght go off.

New Yere had hardlie hitte home
When Arthur telefonede for a Thai takeaway
Loude cryed the laddes for more lagere
Arthur shouted: "Shutte itte! The sprogges are slepen.
Queene Brenda has gotte the arseayke over thyss
She must go to B&Q fyrste thynge, for the Holy Sale
Sir Gary? See if there's any signe of that scranne yet."
But scarcely had Sir Gary got to gardene gayte
When a bigge bastarde on a byke burst inne.
Strayghte up the halle, oil on the Axeminstere
Queene Brenda's Ykea lampe lyinge flatte.
No kyddinge. Thys was a honeye-monstre.
Grene leather, grene leggynges, grene skid-lydde.

Armes lyke legges. Legges lyke tuggebotes
Bigge bushey bearde, down to hys belte buckle
                    strayghte uppe.

            On his bakke a death's head
            Manneres very rude
            And then Sir Gavin said
            "Yow fond of hospital foode?"

The verdant knyght gayve it summe verbal:
"Who's the guv'nor, you bunche of haire-dresseres?"
The Kynge was not best-pleased about thys
And looked about for backuppe from the laddes.
Yet nobody wants a rukke before the nosebagge arryves.
You evere tried Thai takeawaye wyth brokene teethe?
"Anybodie want summe?" Asked the Grene Bykere
"I thought you was supposed to be a harde crewer?"
You coulde see Arthur was just about to loze itte.
Quietly spoke Sir Gawayne: "Outsyde. Ryghte now."
Arthur said: "No, leave itte Wayne." Butte, too layte.
This almyghtie boundle beganne wyth the berque.
Wayne wellied the wlonk wyth a whele-brayce.
Dogge's barkeing. Neigboures' lyghts come on – the lotte.
Thence came the Fylthe. Blues and twos.
                    Wyth backuppe.

The Grene Knyght – and fulle credit too hym, told the Fylthe;
Itte was a misonderstandynge. So offe they trotede.
Then he turned hym round to Gawayne and sayde:
"You. Returne matche. Yeare's tyme. My turfe. Be there.
                    Or else."

            Helmet now wyth dente
            Blood on dayglow veste

Offe the toeragge roared
somewhere to the weste.

Gawayne slinges his Benne Shermanne in the Zanussi
Breakes open a Beckes and belchez lyke a bastarde:
"Thys is well bloodie serious – I'm gonna nede a motore."
Kyng Arthur sayde it woulde be sortede. Saye nomore.
Wynter dragged onne. Then Sprynge and the FA Graile.
Millwalle didn't gette a looke-in. They was robbede.
So the entyre crewe: Arthur, Sir Gawayne, Sir Daerenne
Sir Warrene, Sir Lee, Sir Shaun, Sir Kevinne of New Crosse
And alle the othere johns, flewe to Ibethere for a fought-
                    knyghte's fun.
Muche drinkeing, ruckkinge and horizontale joggeing was there.
Then aftere was deportayscheon and some payeing of fynes.
Soone came Autumne and thenne soddynge Wyntere againe.
Wayne, hys yere neare uppe, must tacqle thys tosssere
The laddes had whyp-rounde beforehonde
Gawayne was gotte in goode ordere by the boyze
Eighteen-hole Docke Martynnes, dodgie mayce gasse.
Combatte kecques, well-sharpenede Stanlye Knyve
Numbere Two croppe, Crombie, Fforde Cortina
The catte's knackeres! For he was well toolede uppe.
"Putte the bastarde out of businez!" Cryed the Kynge.
"Itte's welle in hande. The quaunte's gotte itte comeing."
                    Calles back Gawayne.

The trippe to the northewest as badde as it coulde be
Qontraflowe, roadewerkes and a smacque-uppe by Stoke
Gawayne, as itte goes, endeing uppe neare northe Wayles
Itte was Christemass Eve and he was cremecracquered.
By a stroke of lucke, Gawayne mette anothere mayte
Bertilak, who ranne a garage wyth a knyghtclubbe tacqued onne.
Well-appointeded as itte happenes. Used to runne wyth Arthur.

What a gaffe! Cocquetayle barre. Faerie lyghts. Optiques.
Raisede acrylique shepeskinne dais, smokede glasse tayble.
Waterebedde. And thy was juste the gueste bedroome.
"Staye here as longe as you lyke, Wayne," says Bertilak.
"I know the mushe you're aftere – a right yahoo.
He lives notte two myles from here. Helpe yourselve.
Drynkes. Whatevere. My ladie, Lynette will look aftere you."
Gawayne couldn't believe itte and grateful, he gasps:
"Top geezere!"

Christemasse was kept in a blurre of bier and Bacardie
Gawayne laye in bedde lookeing at Loadede.
Many a locke-in he hadde in Bertilak's barre.
Drynkeing. He gotte completely Schindlere's Liste.
Thenne, three dayes before the bigge battle, Bertilak sayed:
"Oute of Bacardie. I've gotte to go to Cashe & Caerrie.
I'll be backe layter. Mynde the missus for me."
That mornynge, Lynette came into Wayne's chambere.
A handsome tarte. Feistie and fitte-lookeing.
She was tryeing itte onne but Wayne keped coole.
When Bertilak was back, he asked: "Awryghte thenne?"
"Sweete as" goes Wayne. "Sweete as."
Bertilak bungs Wayne a bottele of Bacardie:
"Toppe man. Give *that* summe lewinski thenne."
Welle goode.

Come the next daye. Bertilak drove to Droitwich.
To see a manne about the manifolde on hys motore
Same drill; chill oute, Dude. Helpe yourselve.
Gawayne was wakenede wyth a wet tongue in hys eare.
"Leave itte out Lynette. Yow are Bertilak's beste burde."
By eveninge, Bertilak is back wyth his waftie Y-reg.
"Anythynge happened lyke?" He lokede atte Lynette.

Gawayne buttonede itte, notte wyshing to saye nothynge.

Bertilak bunges hym a boxe of Beckes Biere.

"Sortede thenne."

The thyrd daye, Bertilak beckonns Gawayne, going:

"I've gotte a little tyckle going offe wyth summe tomfoolerie.

Looke aftere Lynette. There'll be a longe drynke in itte layter."

Gawayne is abed whenne Lynette comes inne.

Fulle beautiful, hayre falleing doune, Wonderebra

Legges withoute ende and summe craftie contryvance

Begot from Our Ladie of Janetreger, crotchlesse camiknickeres.

Thys was almoste too muche. Gawayne was gaggeing.

But by prayer to St Clintaune, he kepte hys wyngenutte onne.

He beggede one thynge from hys mayte's missus;

Batteries for his Gaymeboye – flatte since Boxeing Daye.

Thys she gives hym and he settles for a snogge

Wyth no rumtie-tumtie. For thatte was *ryghte* oute.

Thenne Bertilak poppes inne and poures a Pernod.

He gives Gawyane a gold signet ringe for goode lucke.

Lynette loungeing, blissede oute, listeneing to Teddie Pendergrasse.

"Worde inne your shelle-lyke Wayne. Did she trye itte onne?"

"No chaunce."

Nowe dawned the daye of the retourne rukke.

Gawayne gotte into geare, wobblie but welle uppe for itte.

A myle uppe the roade he sees a sign sayeing:

Private Dryve. Keepe Oute. By nowe, he's bricqueing itte.

The Grene Knyghte's garage was huge – a hoogstraaten.

Heareing bangeing from wythin, he warns:

"Come overe here iffe yow thinke you're harde enough."

"Yow slagge." The grebo was giving itte alle of thatte.

"Botelede oute? Yow snowdroppe!" Goes Gawayne.

Thys was takynge the pisse for the Grene Knyght.
He swounge at Wayne's baunce wyth a baysbal batte.
Twyce more he twattede hym. Wayne wouldn'te go doune.
Whenne Wayne, mayced the mushe, itte slowde hym uppe.
But backe he came wyth a kicque to Wayne's criquette-sette.
Which causede Wayne's eyes to welle watere.
"Hadde enough hadde yow? Hadde enough yow bastarde?"
Gawayne grittede hys teethe: "Do yow tayke Swytch?"
                    Theye backked offe.

The Grene Knyght toke hys helmete off hys head
Underneathe itte was Bertilak, Gawayne's hoste.
Gotte uppe lyke a grebo – the fulle maunty
Gawayne gobbesmacqued atte being sette uppe
Kicqued at hys Cortina doore, swearynge stille.
Bertilak said: "Thys wasn't doune to me Wayne.
The Kynge hadde hearde itte said that you was alle mouthe.
He wantede to see howe you cayme uppe inne the washe
But since you're sounde, we'll calle thys a rezulte."
Wyth thatte, the Grene Knyght slung a canne of St Ella
Atte Wayne, who stashede hys Stanlye Knyve awaye.
Thence aftere, theye repayrede to *Gabriella's*
A neareby Knyghtclubbe knowne for lappe-dauncing
Whereuponne theye gayve the shortes a severe caneing
Rezultynge in a rukke wyth seven bounceres
Ande yette anothere runne-inne wyth the locale Bylle.
Bayled oute by Lynette onne Moundaye mornynge
Stille syngng: "No one lykes us. We don't cayre."
                    As itte goes.

Honi Soit Qui Mal y Pense.

A BRIEF HISTORY OF MORSE

Dots and dashes didit didit
Did it in the films
And way out in the woolly west
Awaiting freight from Santa Fe
A marshall in the midday sun
Stands apprehensive with a gun
As sagebrush miles along the track
The buzzards squatting on the poles
Hear signals whisper down the wires
Past cactus, cowskulls, gopher holes
Where tumbleweed goes rolling by
And three bad hombres wait to die.

Dots and dashes didit didit
Did it down the line
When Mister Morse tapped out his test:
"What hath God wrought?"
The question stayed
Unanswered by the snoozing past
Until the future spoke at last
And wagons came.
And men and mines.
Then motor cars and longer lines
Spread out across the yawning land
Till progress had the upper hand.

Dots and dashes didit didit
Did it later on.
In radio blips from storm-tossed ships
Whenever wind and wave kicked up
And hapless vessels in distress
Their flares gone up, gone down, gone out

Still sent a desperate s.o.s
The universal rescue shout.
The dots and dashes didit didit
Did it for so long
It's odd to think they won't be there
Their crotchet/quavers in the air
Dot dot, dot dash – the letter V
The wartime sign for Victory
Was Beethoven's Fifth Symphony
And Samuel Morse's rhapsody
The tune still buried where he hid it
Didit, didit, didit, didit.

THE LOST CHILDHOOD

Let's go in search of childhood
Before it's out of bounds
Or closed to us forever
On health and safety grounds
The scents, the sights, the sounds

Let's bomb across a bombsite
On bikes that have no gears
Where brakes are just for cissies
And tumbles hold no fears
On crossbars of the years

Let's wander over wasteland
And have ourselves a blaze
Of busted laths and pallets
Eyes stinging with a smaze
Of disappearing days

Let's you and I go carting
Get busy with the saw
Bolt the planks and pram-wheels
To struts of two-be-four
Before they change the law

Let's get some nails and axes
Construct a woodland den
Between the spring and winter
Before those council men
Partition Now and Then.

PLACES

The Cycle Path

On a bicycle in winter
Back to Wivenhoe alone
When the smoky Rowhedge rooftops
Through the mist across the Colne
Are forgotten Saxon farmsteads
And the cattle stand like stone
On a still day in December
At the turning of the tide
With the fading roar of traffic
As the Hythe is left behind
For the patterned frosty woodland
Where the leaf veins in the mud
Are the skeletons of fairies
Delicately strewn around
Then the only living sound
Is the wingbeat of a swan
As it flaps its way upriver
Past the moorhens in the sedge
To a white armada waiting
Silent, at the water's edge.

On a bicycle in summer
In the horny pagan heat
Racing with a pleasure steamer
Where the rail and river meet
A woman on the sun-deck
Sees the cyclist on the path
And she smiles, waving madly
Till he disappears in trees
Where the splinters of the sunlight
Splash the hawthorn leaves with gold
And the hollow-way is dappled

Where the burning ball has rolled
When the winter lost a wicket
After spring came in and bowled
A bluebell haze, the smell of rain
The thunder of the London train
A ship's wash jostles driftwood high
The seagulls see the bikes go by
And shriek along the estuary
To Brightlingsea. To Brightlingsea.

THE SHIPYARD

Bramble, Southernwood and Dock
Unsung among the rubble
Were the salvagemen and saviours
Of a shipyard long in trouble:

"Mr Bramble," said his colleague
"Since these premises are ours,
Will you formally confirm it
In the trademark of your flowers?
Now the welders won't return here
And the riveters have gone
We must be about our business
As the summer's getting on."

"Mr Southernwood, the matter
Of this concrete still remains
It may crack with your persistence
A I see you've made some gains
But we fight a losing battle
With the tyrant of the clock

May I venture you prevail upon
The strengths of Mr Dock?"

"Mr Dock, you've made some progress
Since removal of the cranes
If the rusty sun assists us
And the heavy summer rains
We could sign the final papers
And conclude this sorry case
Leaving Mr Moon as watchman
When the winter's on the place."

THE LAST FERRY

When the chestnut slopes are rusty
And the Roman River still
And the reeds the only sentinels
From here to Chopping's Mill
Since the spirits of the legionaries
All returned to Rome
With autumn in the saltings
You will take the ferry home.

The last one of October
And the loneliest of the year
Past blackened ribs of barges
Where the only sound you hear
Is the bickering of seagulls
In a melancholy sky
And the coughing of the engine
At the season sculling by.

Then the swans reclaim the jetty
As the ferry slips from sight
And the sun goes down with jaundice
In a burst of dirty light
Till the shimmer of the windows
From the houses on the hill
Sends a semaphore of sunset
To the crows at Chopping's Mill

And Anchor Hill lies dozing
In the smoke of Sunday fires
And the starlings sit like symphonies
Unplayed upon the wires
And the ferry skipper's silent
At the closing of the day
As the sun creeps out of Quay Street
And the boat is put away.

THE RUINS OF ST PETER'S CHURCH

The ruins of St Peter's Church
Sleep on and twice a month or so
From March until October goes,
An unseen gardener comes to mow
Trims the yews and strims the weeds
And now removes the perished wreaths
Their twisted leaves and rusted wire
To pile upon an autumn pyre
In some quiet corner, well away
From any business of the day

Roofless, open to the sky
The ruins yawn, the clouds go by
The crows and rooks and rabbits pass
Across the floor long-laid to grass.
While ivy on the chancel flowers
On porous Roman brick and lime
The medieval mortar sours
In walls that crumble over time
And overshadow broken crypts
Where winter drags its fingertips

And in the churchyard, overgrown
The women mostly come alone
Bring cloth and brush to clean the stone
Chrysanthemums to deck the urns
Scissors, secateurs and twine
As melancholy at their tasks
They battle briony and bine
On solitary afternoons
Lose themselves in memories
Of husbands, homes, and harvest moons.

Then, once a week, along the track
A cyclist rattles, looking back
Across the furrowed centuries
At quiet familiar things he sees
A ghost parade of country folk
The long-dead farmers and their wives
The spirits in the wayside oak
Where thistledown goes drifting south
Through ruins of St Peter's Church
Towards the silver river mouth

THORRINGTON TIDE MILL

Treading on pedals up Tenpenny Hill
The Brightlingsea buses may find you
Racing the sunset to Thorrington Mill
Only the wind to remind you
The best of the weather's behind you

Tenpenny Brook goes trickling down
Shimmying over the gravel and sand
Turning the tilth of the centuries softly
Sifting the soil with a quicksilver hand

Thorrington Mill sat chugging and churning
Digging a living from out of the mud
Pushing the paddles that milled for the Normans
Scooping the tide which provided her blood

Groaning a protest from deep in her belly
Over the farmland, the barking of dogs
Wallower rolling and chattering damsel
Grinding their teeth went the old wooden cogs

Times when the stonedressers came to the marshes
Sallied from Colchester up to the mill
Journeyman, Master, Apprentice and Boy
Cut into millstone with thrift and its bill

Late after Lammas, with geese in the stubble
Picking the carcass of harvest-time bare
Fruit-weighted hedgerows and summer in trouble
Miller still working and damp in the air

Slackwater days when the mudflats go silver
Late, like a lord deep in debt, comes the sun
Peering past trees in the haze of September
Dusty old windows of Thorrington Mill
Waiting for wagons from Tenpenny Hill.

THE GRIMY WONDERS OF THE WORLD

The old industrial spectres rattle
Heavy chains on Pennine scars
And groan to be forgiven
By the grey-black grimy hills
But among those mines and mills
Lay the forge of western wealth
Where the lesions healed slowly
If at all, until by stealth
Time and nature petrified
The iron mastodons and rust
Rain or ruin dragged the monsters
Down to rubble, shale or dust.

And dirty docks and hulking wharfs
Which witnessed sailing ships come in
Saw holds picked clean by locust cranes
Heard hoists and hawsers creak and keen
While in the country in between
The thrumming ports which burgeoned then
And reeking towns, huge gangs of men
Built long canals which served as veins
To feed their filthy throbbing hearts
Until the coming of the trains.

With Cornish tin, Mancunian cotton
Sheffield steel and Stafford plates
And everything the British made
The tables of the world were laid.

And all these towers and blackened walls
Great edifices leering down
Those bridges built by engineers
Their soot-thick girders linking town
With latticed iron to other town
Will have to do for pyramids
Our Hanging Gardens, Colossi,
A last remaining memory
Of times when giants strode the land
And what we had –
Was industry.

ANTHEM FOR ESSEX

Tilty, Wimbish, Stebbing, Shopland
Chipping Ongar, Ingatestone
All the market towns and hamlets
On the rivers Crouch or Colne
West of Walton, east of Easton
Shellow Bowells to Hanningfield
London's bread-bin, lungs and love-nest
Beaches, birdland, wood and weald
Essex. Seaxes, sheaves and shield.

Here the horsemen met for racing
Here the highwaymen were hung

Here the painter saw the skyline
Here the tide would poke its tongue
In among the samphire saltings
While the sun set sea alight
Here the smugglers moved the malmsey
Up the creek in dead of night
Customs cutter out of sight.

Saucy, sexy, seaside Essex
Driest place in British Isles
Where the robbers took retirement
When the Sweeney shut the files
Home of rock and naughty rhythms
Pirates, Paramounts and Procul
Harum, Hotrods, Ian Dury
Dr Feelgood – they were local
With Lee Brilleaux on lead vocal.

Epic Essex, best for bike-rides
Liberally laced with lanes
Pubs to punctuate the pedalling
Flower-baskets hung on chains
Coastal Essex – secret rivers
Heron-haunted waterland
Where the silver light in autumn
Lingers for a saraband
On the shingle and the sand.

Here are tales of long-dead writers,
Ghostly bikers, missing planes
Council gardens, scrapyards, thatches
Cricket matches seen from trains
Yellow fields in dazzled springtime
Varnished by a Van Gogh sky

Blind the copses and the spinneys
Where the rooks are building high
And the world goes skating by.

Where the weather-boarded cottage
Waits in moddy monochrome
Nestling with new commuters
And the future coming home
Envious London, stuck in traffic
Simmering its quiet desires
Senses Essex spanning endless
Hazier than orchard fires
Out beyond those distant spires.

Our Part In The Class War

Yer grandad was a Green Line bus driver
Left school at fourteen. Called Gran 'The Guvnor.'
and before he biked off to work at the garridge,
he used to take her a cup of tea up in bed.
Milk bottle on the tea-table, eggs and bacon for breakfast
and gave the plate to the dog to lick.
Came home for his dinner at lunchtime.
Read a good deal and listened to the wireless a lot.

Rented a terraced house for nearly all of his life.
Kept a couple or three beers in the sideboard
with yer gran's Bristol Cream and his toffees.
Wore a weskitt down the garden, Saturdays
kept a pencil behind his ear and mucked about
in the shed while yer gran peeled the spuds
squinting, a Kensitas hanging from her mouth.

Tin o' salmon in case o' visitors. Toast'n'dripping
for supper, *some* Sunday nights. If you brought a
girl home, it was a 'cooked tea'. Swiss Roll & Evap
for pud. Not 'sweet'. Not 'dessert'. Pud. You didn't
come across garlic, granary bread, sea-salt or
a pepper-mill till you were almost twenty.

The coal cupboard used to be in the kitchen.
An outside toilet. Not loo. Not lav. Never; khazi.
On Monday mornings, Gran boiled the hankies
in a special saucepan and threw the lodger's
socks out the top window. *He* did the front garden
in his shirtsleeves on a Sunday – which had been
a bit controversial in its time. You were amazed
if you went round to a schoolfriend's for tea and
they had a breakfast room. Or a study. Or a
garden big as Hampshire. And not a long flinty
strip, with conker-tree staves for beansticks.

If company came round, the kettle went on and
the telly went off. Occasionally, he spat on the fire
and he always pickled his own onions. Weekends
and holidays he let you stay up late. Then he said:
"Come on now Cocker. Clean yer railings, then up
them wooden hills to Bedfordshire" You never
heard him describe himself as working class.
It wasn't the sort of thing he went on about.

NEW ENGLISH LANDSCAPES

Their names are English names, the hills
Inscrutable through sheets of rain
Stay sulking under clouds until
The spotlight sun comes out again
To trace the trickles on their spines
Of rushing becks from ironstone mines
That wend and widen down the lea
To feed the farms that skirt the sea.

Their names are English ones – and old:
Tinwistle, Longstone, 'down' or 'wold'
Some Saxon lad or Norseman came
To hang each landmark with its name
When gazing from an autumn hill
While gales stripped a rusting wood
He never thought: "A science park
– or football stadium might be good."

Too soon the rumbling lorries come
The worker ants with safety hats
The cranes the diggers and the pipes
The planners and the technocrats
Put up some dreadful edifice
A deal done behind closed doors
By coffee-quaffing metro-yobs
Who specialise in bending laws.

The wind won't dawdle on the moors
The Wordworths and the Brontes knew
But slices down the carriageway
To chill the ministers today

And those locations on their maps
Their names are English names, I'm told.
Which won't mean much to busy chaps
Tinwistle, Longstone, 'down' or 'wold'.

MY OWN NORTH-SOUTH DIVIDE

I have worked and wandered
in this land they call the North
Wolfed breakfast on grey Sunday
in a dark pub, back of Bury
Sat on trams on Saturdays
and snaked through brick-black cities
Stood on cliffs in Cleveland
seen Upleatham under snow
Cycled over Saddleworth
and drunk a pint in Dukinfield
Milled in Morrisons and mingled
with the crowds at Ashton Market
Sang at Builders, Huddersfield
and crashed in a council house
in Mixenden, surrounded by
the hoary, hardworked hills of Halifax
Sat in Harry Ramsden's eating
perfect chips. Drank perfect pints
No less than a two inch head.

I've had my tea in Harrogate
Walked the coal-seam beach at
Salburn, gone to Guisborough
by bus, seen Roseberry Topping
Walked by graffiti wheelie-bins

by numerous grimy back-to-backs
named after old Crimean battles
Seen the Tees from Southbank
and Middlesbrough burning
in the sulphur-amber night.
Wandered into lunchtime market
pubs, where dark-eyed beehive
barmaids called me 'Luv'
Watched sodden Cumbrian collies
working, sat on trains in pouring rain
from Leeds to Northallerton
And having heard the red hat
and no knickers of it all
A different land, is what I thought
Being southern and no better
than I ought.

RIVER TO RIVER

The River Colne meanders slow
Through fecund farmlands, rainy green
A ribbon strewn across the floor
Of shallow valleys, hardly seen
Or guessed at from the Essex shore

East to Colchester and on
Its ullages and spillages
The houses and their secrets tucked
In hamlets and the villages
Around the Chappel viaduct

To Fordstreet, Fordham Bridge it goes
And idles by the Essex Way
Strengthened by St Botolph's Brook
It sidles by the road to pay
Its namesake Roman town a look

Widening there, it picks up speed
Skirting fields towards the mill
Where it stopped to pay a tithe
Beside the bridge below the hill
Before it hurried to The Hythe

Haggling with the tide for business
When the ships sailed up the Colne
Galleys, luggers, barges, smacks
Buildings plonked like Toblerone
Where they once unloaded sacks

Now the new estates are fronting
Toytown wharfs that dwarf the marshes
Wivenhoe and Brightlingsea
Wearing them like false moustaches
Edging up the estuary

Here the Saxon Sea comes hacking
While the River Colne expands
Mersea Flats and Cocum Hills
Gazing south to Maplin Sands
Where the biggest river spills

Now the blood of other rivers:
Crouch, Blackwater, Medway, Swale
Mingle, eddy, dash the shoreline
As container cargoes sail
Round the Thames's yawning jawline

Shimmying up that serpent river
Go the humble and the great
– Other rivers' sons and daughters,
While the bouncers on the gate:
Kent and Essex, watch the waters

Coalhouse Point to Richmond Lock
Galleon's Reach to Watney's Brewery
Flotsam, jetsam, oil and beer
Hogarth sits with Ian Dury
Dreaming Cherry Garden Pier

Underneath that dirty duvet
Of the sky, the river swells
Carrying simple craft to fame
In a carillon of bells
Drowning others in its shame.

Carrying sons of Colne to London
With a daubing or a ditty
To the busy landing stages
And the currents of the city
As it has throughout the ages.

THE GOODS TRAIN

Her undercarriage thunders low
Above a rusty ragweed track
A freight train out of Felixstowe
A full mile long she'll rumble back
And having smelt the Suffolk sea
The long flat fields that clad the fens
She'll grumble into Midlands yards
"It's on the cards, it's on the cards."

With sea containers, iron ore
And pine to stack a timber store
Or minerals and merchandise:
Egyptian spuds, Basmati Rice
And all her network none the worse
For Dr Beeching's creaking curse
She'll whistle at the Midlands moon:
"Returning soon, returning soon!"

She pauses in a passing-loop
To let the Intercity through
While somewhere near a chicken coop
A cockerel queries "What's to do?"
When dawn comes over, slouching by
To drape itself across the sky
She sends the waiting day a text:
"Nuneaton next. Nuneaton next."

Impatient till the journey ends
With stations packed, commuters grave
A whiff of steel and diesel blends
With coffee, bagels, aftershave

They're in a daze – or dozing there
Till mournful on the Midlands air
She wails to say she's coming through
"Heart of England – much to do!"

THE LAST OF THE GREASY SPOONS

In a low-slung shack along the coast
Where men in vests wolf beans on toast
Here's Jan, your waitress, Reg, your host
In the last of the greasy spoons.

Where tea comes steaming from an urn
A darker shade of tan we learn
Its strength will be the main concern
In the last of the greasy spoons.

The sugar's white, the sauce is brown
Tomatoes tinned – then rendered down
Low calorie? Get outta town.
It's last of the greasy spoons.

For a fuller figure than Posh Spice
We recommend the two fried slice
Black pudding, chips – let's make that twice
In the last of the greasy spoons.

Where smoking is a discipline
Permitted everywhere within
With ashtrays fashioned out of tin
In the last of the greasy spoons.

Unvisited by Tony Blair
No Tuscan fragrance scents the air
They'll never serve polenta there
In the last of the greasy spoons.

You won't find Wedgewood Blue or Spode
Though Catering White is a la mode
For blokes who turn in off the road
To the last of the greasy spoons.

Where fearsome men with hams for hands
Mouth asterisks and ampersands
At knackered fops who play in bands
In the last of the greasy spoons.

That wholefood franchise shall not pass
Neurotics nibbling blades of grass
They'll never know the working class
Like the last of the greasy spoons.

THE DARK SIDE

Horses Seen Through Trees

Some silver autumn morning
Remember days like these
As horses seen through trees.

And in forgotten orchards
The ochre of the sun
And echo of a gun

A gale bends the birches
The elders crick and groan
The moon is smashed to pieces
In waters of the Colne
And autumn drags you home.

The dead are reacquainted
With living they have known
Their half-remembered faces
In flowers, moss and stone
Ashes, earth or bone.

And if I die in early autumn
Light a fire boy – in the woods
Build it well and crack a bottle
Share out all my worldly goods

And on some silver morning
Remember days like these
As horses seen through trees.

The Funeral of a Young Man

Wakes Colne, White Colne
Earls Colne and Colne Engaine
Rain-washed green in early summer
As I cycle home again
Past the Chappel viaduct
Only memories will remain
Wakes Colne, White Colne
Earls Colne and Colne Engaine.

At the church, St Peter's Halstead
Cycle oil on trouser leg
Hymns were hardly made to measure
Service strictly off-the-peg
"Always worse, when it's a young man."
Wheezed an older woman's voice
Yes, I thought – a decent send-off
Pay your money, take your choice
Sleep forever in the graveyard
At the eastern edge of town
Toxic yew trees, raised umbrellas
English weather – pouring down.

He'd been chef and I'd been porter
Fond of cricket, kind to me
Strange the things that you remember;
Liked a song by Kiki Dee
Working in a narrow kitchen
Deafened by the radio
Shouted jokes and muddled orders
"Table five? Away you go!"

Different blokes on different wages
Makes me sorry, now I think
He was bringing up a family
I was spending mine on drink.

He'd been ill – I got a phone call
Now I'm cycling in the rain
Wakes Colne, White Colne
Earls Colne and Colne Engaine
Had to borrow shirt and jacket
He'd be laughing like a train
Wakes Colne, White Colne
Earls Colne and Colne Engaine.

Nineteen miles from home to Halstead
Nineteen miles, then back again
Had the notion that exertion
Might stave off potential pain
Coming home, I passed a postman
And we spoke, as cyclists will
Asked me, was I in a hurry?
Only to be living still.

Past the Chappel viaduct
Only memories *can* remain
Wakes Colne, White Colne
Earls Colne and Colne Engaine.

Poor Mohammed's Daughter

Mohammed's fillings, buccal and occlusal
In gaping mouth, when he throws back his head
Confirm the diligence of Baghdad dentists
If not the fact his little daughter's dead
This picture of the grocer is unusual
His howling anguish, shock and disbelief
The intimacy, wedded to intrusion.
A war allows us windows on such grief

In eastern England now, the spring advances
A sharp east wind still nibbles at the days
In Colchester, the soldiers' pubs stay empty
As field-by-field the farmland turns to baize
The rooks are building higher, which enhances
The chance that summer comes up with the goods
The sergeants' wives must exercise the dogs now
They hear the transport planes above the woods

A gung-ho newsman on the television
In self-important bullying semi-dark
With barely-bridled relish, talks of tactics
Astride a giant model of Iraq
A line of virtual tanks take up position
And flash up gold explosions on attack
In science can put missiles through a cat-flap
It won't bring poor Mohammed's daughter back

In Babylon, they've cluster bombs not towers
In Nineveh, not quinquereme but Bradley
Where hope dissolves in nausea and migraine
The ancient world is doing rather badly
The children of the modern world spend hours

With drips in arms and bandages on heads
And 'surgical' are strikes – which does seem clearer
Observing tiny patients on their beds

"You betcha melted boots we're coming, mister.
A war is best held fresh or it'll spoil
You gotta go in hard to burst a blister
Especially if that blister's full of oil."
Poor Mohammed held his daughter, kissed her
Brushed the blood and dust from matted hair
Noting that her body seemed much lighter
Never seeing the camera clicking there.

NEW MALTHUSIANS

Cranefly-thin comes Africa
Its begging bowl held up before
The acetone of starving breath
Which sighs on Europe's fortress door
From marching wraiths of rainless plains
All swaddled pale in dusty gauze
The skeletons of stillborn states
Will scratch the walls with bony claws

We waddle through the shopping malls
Burn lights all day, eat fuel all night
In sleepless greed with anxious eyes
On adverts which assert our right
To grain and petrol. Petrol/grain
The rich man's crop, the fat man's pride
The boardroom sits and shrugs its hands
An old equation pushed aside

The east will breed, the west must shop
What Malthus dares to raise his voice
Against the witless appetites
Of freedom, travel, sex or choice?
With barn half-empty, stocks gone down
As boats return from catchless seas
The farmer hears the low-pitched hum
Of locusts on a searing breeze

The shadow of the wealthy falls
Obscures the light and keeps at bay
The facts too hard to countenance
On continents too far away
And while the water-wasting west
Will witter on about its diet
A wind whips up around its walls
But Malthus – if he's there, keeps quiet.

THE LAST BOYS IN THE WOODS

August, tinder dry
The woods belong to me
The wind, the magpies and the lazy sun
And all the boys have grown up and are gone
John, three years away
And Will on soldier's pay
And Steven building boats in Brightlingsea
And Simon, lost his mind to LSD.

The kids now longer come
Cos fearful Dad or Mum
Reminded by the news of violent ends

Now chauffeur them by car to visit friends
No boyish voices sing
No camping kettles ring
The treehouse Simon built when he was well
Is long-abandoned now, and empty shell.

All these lads were good
The last boys in the wood
I listen for their voices, there are none.
Just me, the wind, the magpies
Me, the wind, the magpies
Me, the wind, the magpies and the sun
And all the sacred innocence is gone.

THE DEATH OF NELSON

In that autumnal Norfolk sky
Its vastness mirroring the seas
The mainsail clouds which overfly
The deck-flat fields and mizzen trees
Horatio, the sickly son
Of Rector Nelson's dying wife
Will take on board his soul's supplies
The totems of a later life

Viscount Nelson Of The Nile
His quarter-profile staring out
With solemn lips which yield no smile
The soulful English eyes, no doubt
A face with very few regrets
And if his stance – the sword at side
The frogging and the epaulettes –

Diverts the gaze, it cannot hide
A flat and pinioned empty sleeve
The boyish lightness of a frame
Which enemies, on viewing it
Won't tally with the weighty name

But Nelson at the end is dead
The battle of Trafalgar won
A murderous cough of smoke and lead
Expectorated at the sun
A sniper's bullet in his spine
Across the orlop deck he lies
England in the mainsail clouds
Reflected in his faded eyes
The mizzen trees, the autumn seas
And vastness of those Norfolk skies

Then from the Spanish waters, north,
Preserved in brandy, bring him home
And bear his shattered body forth
To Paul's Cathedral and its dome
Which looms across the gun-grey Thames
The day the cheerless funeral dawns
Where cranes salute the wooden ships
And all of England's navy mourns.

THE SCORE

Ordinary boys they were –
Simple lads gone out to play
Footie in the local park
Weather not too hot that day

Boys, the news reiterated
Ten to fifteen years, no more
Little worlds they have at
that age.
Only football dreams
The score.

As the great Euphrates squeezes
Past Ramadi, feeds the lake
Forks in two, meandering on
South south-east to Babylon
Biblical this land
You could say
Ground well-steeped in
wasted blood
Wadis thirsting for the deluge
March to Maytime in the flood
When the delta turns to mud

Hardly more than children really.
Kickabout mere minutes in
When the bomb went off
beside them.
Rubble. Screaming.
Statement. Spin.
Eighteen young Iraqi Beckhams
Urchins versus Dogs of War
Look away now.
Look away now
You don't want to know
the score.

GIN LANE 2007

Among the running footsteps
The roar of ape or bear
A whiff of rank testosterone
Hangs acrid on the air
Where shiny blondes
with muddy eyes
Stand freezing in a line
Screeching into mobiles
In a fog of Calvin Klein

In gutters clogged with debris
The dog-ends die like stars
A charmer headbutts windows
As bouncers hulk by bars
A minibus of policemen
Sit tensely, settled down
A night become a lifetime
In every country town

A drunkard pays a sergeant
In epithets he's polished
A song for sozzled England
In key of B Demolished
The shirt he put on earlier
Bloody, though still pressed
The evidence, material
A change led to arrest

As William Hogarth's spirit
Looks on in recognition
In A&E, the standard:
Another stabbed admission

A headache in the morning
And shovelling to do
Bladdered for a penny
Murderous drunk for two.

THE WEATHER BACKCAST

Late one winter night
With the rain lashing down outside
I woke up with the video tape still running
The detritus of an evening-in all around me
The remote. The full ashtray. The empty bottles.
When suddenly, on the TV screen
Was an ancient weather forecast
From some long-forgotten summer
Maybe four or five years earlier
The weather-girl looked suntanned
She spoke of clear August nights
And how bright the stars would be tonight
That we could expect some early morning mist
Lingering in certain low-lying areas
Which would soon be burned off by the sun
She said that it would be another hot day
With a pleasant cooling breeze on the coast

And I thought of working outside
And the records playing on the radio then
And walking along the still-warm pavements
After work, to go dusty into a shop
We knew different people in those days
I brought my wages home to another kitchen
The pub was roaring, juke-box blasting

Blokes with money, work – and work to come.
The women cheerful, tipsy and flirty
Some brilliant forgotten summer before the split
And so. Still out-of-it, I go to the front door
And the rain and the freezing wind desolate me
And I'll tell you this much:
You never really know what you've got
Till it's gone.

THE NORTH SEA

This is the sea the sailor saw
Which thrashed the shingle on the shore
Swallowed sloops and galleons whole
Yet gave up herrings by the shoal
The 'silver treasure' called by men
Built Blythburgh – a fish church then
Paid for its windows and chimeres
Though took back Dunwich in arrears

This is the sea of winter geese
Its gun-grey, bird-limed, heaving fleece
The Whale Road where the Saxons went
To settle Suffolk, Essex, Kent.
Cold currents fetched the codfish down
Filled ketches, smacks and fed the town
And sped the skillingers to bring
The oysters back from Terschelling

This was a sea of working ways
Of dirty, bleach-stained denim days
Where little ships from net-strewn quays

Their halliards rattling in the breeze
Set out with men in set-jawed mood
To turn their labours into food
Who knew, when fishing quotas bit
That nothing good could come of it

This was a sea of fish and birds
And all the figures, facts and words
On how its creatures disappear
Cannot convey its troubles here
– Nor any pious why-oh-whying.
The sea, the old North Sea is dying
And muffles in its warming swell
The tolling of the Dunwich bell.

A Pop Star Falls From Grace

So how was there no safety net?
And what will they be thinking now?
The fans who screamed your name
At clubs and supermarket openings
The friendly policemen helping you
To swan past queues where doormen
Dropping cordons, waved you through.

The make-up girls and cameramen
Who can no longer tell their friends
They worked with you, remember you.
The pop reporters whom you knew
Have long moved on to higher things
Confessionals or football books
And retrospectives, not including *you*.

Once-envious hometown workmates
Are grateful that they chose a normal life
And never had that supernatural drive
Which fuels ambition – and odd appetites.
Though one or two, in backstreet pubs
May mention confidentially, in passing
That they'd often felt you weren't quite right

Now former agents, managers
And fellow stars aren't taking calls
It's difficult. They hope you'll understand.
While posters of much fresher boys
Adorn their long-redecorated walls
Names of clubs have all been changed
And evidence removed from play-lists

Marooned in a Job-Centre interview
Asked what your last employment was
You hear a whistling from another room
And notice that it's one of your old hits.
Then in a further highlight of that week
Your bored and faintly pitying GP
Refers his observations to your lawyer

Hood pulled up and tranquilised
In a van back to the accommodation
You ask yourself over and over:
So how was there no safety net?
How was there no safety net?
How was there no safety net?
How?

A Return
To Flanders

ONE

In dust of this museum
Lit dully by the sun
The specks like tiny planets
Go drifting one by one
The souls of sleeping soldiers
Suspended in their prime
Who heard the bells of Arras
And settled, after time.

Troop dutifully by now
Exhibits of the years
The mortar shells and badges
The pay-books in arrears
The trenching spades and buckles
Of sergeants and recruits
Who left their rusting helmets
Their billy-cans and boots

Historians and poets
Re-published over years
Appended and amended
The inventory of tears
The irony remains though
Despite all items crossed:
Because of human progress
Eight million lives were lost

Though don't let's haggle on it
Of how it was begun
Or how the hun killed Tommy
Or Tommy killed the hun
Not in this French museum

Lit dully by the sun
In dust of all these decades
The two are now at one.

TWO

In Federal yellow, Euro blue
The trains snake out from Waterloo
And chug along the weed-choked track
On south-east London's unscrubbed back
They glide beside the downs of Kent
The gentle way the troop trains went
Eventually dropping south
To halt outside the tunnel-mouth
And after varying lengths of wait
Leave England by her picket gate
Till twenty minutes on, about
The whole of Europe opens out
Then casually, yawns and yields
The unexciting Flanders fields
Grown over long-corroded guns
And crusted blood of all her sons
Where on damp mornings, locals said
The land still stinks – not of the dead
In bone-flecked furrows everywhere –
But rusting iron on the air.

It's not the France of those with means
For pantiled gites in magazines
Though Arras is a pretty town
The English herd moves further down
South-west or more south-east it ambles

Almost like… it *sensed* the shambles
Quaint idea, though errant stuff
It simply isn't warm enough
And Flanders is notorious
The farming work laborious
Its common catch-crop, lead and iron
Of German eagle, British lion
A cannon-shell, a wagon wheel
They lost along the road to Lille
The workers taciturn, sincere
Eschewing wine for Flemish beer
Are almost English in their looks
And rarely grace the tourist books
Though in the summer every year
The thinning ranks of chaps appear
Who stand sea-eyed to gaze once more
Remembering a later war.

THREE

November hangs on winter
Like bodies hang on wire
Exhausted on the tree boughs
A last few leaves expire
While wreaths of paper poppies
Run pink in dripping rain
The ghosts of broken soldiers
Are waiting for a train.

The melancholy generals
With Marshall Foch respond
In grunts and nods and thank-yous

The forest of Rethondes
Near Compiègne is chosen
Three days they'll wrangle there
Their trains sat in the sidings,
To sign the Clairière

Eleven/eleven/eleven
This peace made on a train
To spare the weary living
And stem the flood of slain
Who swamped the fields of Flanders
Picardy and Champagne
Restoring to the farmers
Their livelihood again.

The trenches, pits and craters
Abandoned as they'd been
The hue of blood and faeces
And not a patch of green
The rats grown fat on corpses
On ground the gas made sour
And not a tree left standing
And not a single flower…

FOUR

When I was ten – or not much more
In 'sixty-three or 'sixty-four
The damage of the First World War
Was still around, I sometimes saw
A tramp with medals on his chest
Though destitute, he did his best

He marched, more than he walked around
But startled by a sudden sound
– A car backfiring in the town,
He'd panic, throw his body down
Clap filthy hands across his ears
And tremble or dissolve in tears
Some nameless terror in his head
"Poor sod," the passing shoppers said
Being kinder then, perhaps, than now
Conveyed it to us kids somehow:
"It's shell-shock – from the war, you see."
And whispered later on to me:
"The last war yielded far more dead
"But oh, the First was worse," they said.

The Great War, whether right or wrong
Although it cast its shadow long
Its winning cultured no conceit
No Vimy, Somme or Ypres Street
Became a London thoroughfare
There is no Paschendaele Square
If other conflicts lend their name
To roads and highways, all the same
The Great War left the streets alone
Inhabiting a darker zone
Of gaps in families, seeds unsown
Of fathers, uncles, names unknown
Of meetings never reconvened
Of debts unsettled, slates uncleaned
The breaking of that simple thread
Which binds the living to the dead
And sombre, some November day
With trees outlined against the grey
The country stops, observes the date
And rakes the embers in its grate.

FIVE

At Ipswich Square in Arras
An English phone box sits
The British fought two battles
The town was left in bits
And further, through an alley
The Place des Héros funnels
Into a larger, grander square
With labyrinthine tunnels

The Spanish-Flemish grandeur
Of centuries before
The pockmarked sandstone pillars
Were skittled during war
Estaminets and churches
Destroyed in occupation
Restored with patient labour
And German compensation

The tunnels under Arras
And cellars where they ended
Were utilised, adapted
Developed and extended
By Scots and Maori soldiers
Who worked them much like mines
And dug for stifling, dripping miles
Beneath the German lines

They lived… *existed* down here
Cooked food and carved crude faces
Into the claustrophobic chalk
Of sundry stopping places
And left their names and countries

Bashed out with maul and knife
Perhaps to help remind them
There'd been an earlier life.

SIX

When China Wright and Charlie Newell
Were young, the world had thinner gruel
Than most of us are dished today
And both were posted long away
The first to Egypt – lucky chance
The second out to northern France
While China quietly did his bit,
Charlie, in the thick of it
– A medic, joined six years before –
Would see a rather rougher war
My grandads: ordinary chaps
The yeomanry this country taps
If ever there's a song and dance
Would take up arms and then advance
And Charlie, never one to wait
Who re-enlisted 'thirty-eight
Was posted back abroad once more
A V2 hit a Woolworths store…
His boys were told their mum was dead
He drank himself to death, they said.

"A pint of wallop and a job
A girl at home, an extra bob
To put by for a rainy day."
As China had been known to say
Was all that they expected then

An England, full of youngish men
Whom war made prematurely old,
Asked what they did, they joked: "As told."
And winked and called each other "cock"
Kept pubs, drove buses, watched the clock
Anonymous in caps they wore
Brought up polite, they seldom swore
In front of children or their wives
They rented houses all their lives
And bodgered in their sheds for years
With pencil stubs behind their ears
A now-forgotten breed of blokes
Whose stubborn ways and arcane jokes
So hard to re-communicate
Were what made Britain quietly great.

SEVEN

So Tommy put his mask on
As someone banged the gong
He heard the thump of gas shells
Like footballs landing wrong
And men began to panic
And shouted it was gas
And prayed the wind would waft it
Away towards Arras

He later saw the corpses
Laid out on frozen mud
All lemon-yellow, lolling tongues
Their nostrils clogged with blood
While medics fixed the blindfolds

To choking, crying men
Who one week out of Blighty
Went sightless home again

Young Harry checked his privates
A bullet went beneath
He never felt the second one
Which entered through his teeth
So Tommy manned the fire-step
And hauled the corpse about
To supplement the sandbags
A shell had blasted out

And stretchered back to England
On trucks and railway tracks
He thought about young Harry
The mustard gas attacks
The sandbags made of bodies
The faces – which were worse
Then lost control completely
And threw up on a nurse.

EIGHT

The clock that chimes on market day
When heard from this estaminet
Sounds pretty as it marks the time
Reminding of a nursery rhyme
The Place des Héros and Grand' Place
The ancient quarters of Arras
Have seen more soldiers on their stones
– Young men who'd never make old bones –

And echoed to that marching sound
Than almost anywhere around.
The Romans and the Spanish came
And left, though Arras took her name
A word from Celtic: Water – *Ar*
The locals, known as *Arageois*
Who dealt in tapestries and lace
Were used to strangers in the place
Knew bloodshed in the market square
And spawned a son called Robespierre
Who made a name himself one day
By setting guillotines in play.

In fields which surround this town
A quarter-million troops went down
Those modern European sons
Who, torn from families, given guns
Were wounded, died, went missing there
– Just atomised, in Flanders air –
Were caught on wire or drowned in mud
Or shot like dogs or choked on blood
Till many who survived the war
Would ask what they were fighting for
And was it worth this bloody mess?
Back would come the answer: "Yes."
Of course, as Bertolt Brecht would say:
"War is like love – it finds a way."
Until at last we all see sense
Our names shall go on monuments
And death retain its dark romance
Despite the fact we die like ants
As men at desks insist we must
– Until we are museum dust.

NINE

In towns of eastern England
Like Framlingham or Diss
They'd always pack the churches
Around the Armistice
A brass band in the High Street
To honour all those men
Though, church was quiet at Easter
They all played football then

The Catchpoles and the Thurgoods
From field, farm and forge
The sacrifice of Suffolk
For Plumer, Haig and George
Who never asked a question
And only owned one suit
Yet put the thing on gladly
And crowded to recruit

They all rushed off to Flanders
To Flanders, in the rain
To give what-for to Fritzi
Then pop back on the train
They'd all be done by Christmas
And back in civvy hats
The heads of huns in helmets
As bully-beef for rats

So from this French museum
Lit dully by the sun
Pick up the glossy leaflets
The tour has just begun
The Battlefields tomorrow

And former Siegfried line
The Beffroi chimes the hour
A coach departs at nine.

TEN

The train glides back to Waterloo
In Federal yellow, Euro blue
As autumn loiters in the park
At five o'clock already dark
The clocks gone back, the days drawn in
A woman with her poppy tin
Her iron hair and winter hat
Goes home and trembles in her flat
The shellburst in the sky she fears
And those explosions which she hears
Are not the fireworks seen outdoors
But rolling thunder of two wars
Carried on the wind and rain
Over from a Flanders plain

They'll cough beside the Cenotaph
The great and good and chiefs-of-staff
While wreaths are laid and words are said
And everyone will bow their head
Acknowledging, in general gloom
The unknown warrior's empty tomb
He's there because, we must assume
The *actual* dead take too much room
The need arose, the men would fight
Like Charlie Newell and China Wright
And everybody that they knew

And every other bugger too.
So war retains its dark romance
Despite the fact we die like ants
As men at desks insist we must
Until we are museum dust.

TIMES AND
SEASONS

New Year's Eve

The old year shifted
Plain as that
It slunk out, like a tired old cat
Ridged of spine and dull of eye
As waning in a windy sky
The last of thirteen moons
passed by
Unseen by celebrating crowds
In semaphore behind the clouds

Though on the keening wind
The sounds
of clinking glass
And whoops and cheers
And hooters
From the lonely ships
Veterans of nameless trips
On rivers run through
other years
Reverberated in the ears

And over frosty football fields
The rockets hissing in the rain
And churchbells wrestled
with the gale
Fading in and out again
Till in the spindly hands
of trees
Like unpicked fruits
And one by one

The birds called out
the milky sun
And thus,
a new year was begun.

NOT AN ORDINARY LOVE

It isn't hearts and flowers that I remember
But the rosehip bridges of September
A fading clip and clop of platform clogs
The frosty terraced streets and secret snogs
Splintered benches where we used meet
The windy ginnels, February sleet
The bus-rides over hills to drab cafes
In market towns on winter Saturdays
Taking all account of push and shove
Ours was not an ordinary love.

And working for a living at sixteen
Started young back then, we did, I mean
They don't these days – it's not encouraged now
Growing up seemed sooner then, somehow
It isn't Valentines though, I remember
But foggy evening lanes in late November
You in scoop-necks, me in baggy trousers
Staring at the rich folk in their houses
Plotting Premium Bond-wins, hand-in-glove
Ours was not an ordinary love.

– Nor an ordinary time at that
Your first driving lesson, my first flat
Three floors up, the bath, if you were willing

For a one-hour wait and had a shilling
'Seventies – it doesn't seem that long
What was that old Paul McCartney song?
C-Moon. Close to Christmas d'you recall
Arguing outside about it all?
Tears. And then the making of it right.
A far from ordinary night.

And all the words I said, I meant and more.
To hang around as woodsmoke at your door
Till early spring, a promise on the breeze
The hazy green that ghosts across the trees
And fields waking up, on days like these
Then later, with the outdoor work begun
You, on a country station in the sun
Waiting on a Friday for the train
To bring your dusty boyfriend home again
Cheerful, after drinking with the guv
Ours was not an ordinary love.

Both of us at work – hard work as such
Twenties, you don't think about it much
Labourer and waitress of renown
Get stuck in, get paid and hit the town
Sod the others and their cold ambition
Were we not in love? We had a mission:
Have a brilliant time before we lost it.
Not sit down with abacus to cost it
In event of judgment from above.
Ours was not an ordinary love.

As I said, it wasn't hearts and flowers
Rescuing Rapunzels from their towers
But an atmosphere of stolen hours

Idle shelter from those sudden showers
In museums, like paupers at a ball
Staring at the grandness of it all
Raincoat pockets, ticket stubs and tissues
In those carefree days were all our issues
Shabby pigeon and his scruffy dove
Ours was not an ordinary love.

Never big occasions I remember
But the skint nights-in around December
One bar of a three-bar gas-fire hissing
Lovers on an indoor sunbreak, kissing
Kitchen-trips for optional excursions
Making tea or switching on immersions
Caught by tipsy test card, unawares
Squaring to the challenge of the stairs
After taking stock of their location
Ours was not an average situation .

Pop-star posters peeling on the wall
That's what I remember most of all
In the kitchen. making home-made wine
Quite forgot about the valentine
You due home in minutes, from your shift
Had to knock one up – and rather swift
Cardboard, paper, scissors and the glue
"Here's a new-wave Valentine for yo-ou!"
Blackmail typeface from a velvet glove
Ours was not an ordinary love.

We never did the jet set stuff – not us
We opted for the railway or the bus
Over autumn moorlands to the sea
Round the ruined castle and some tea

Backstreet book-exchanges then a beer
Ironstone gorges, waterfall and weir
Beaches out-of-season, groynes and dunes
Marram grass and sandy afternoons
Westerlies to give the clouds a shove
Ours was not an ordinary love.

Not the trifling trinkets that I bought you
But the courage which it took to court you
Having saddled up and got that far
Was I not your Co-Op Lochinvar?
You, my Happy Shopper Queen of Sheba?
Hair by *Icarus* and eyes by *Biba*
Aramis for me, *Kĩku* for you
Fragrant then, if nothing else, we two.
Wrapped around each other when as supple
This was not an ordinary couple.

This was not an ordinary caper
And it never made the local paper
In the pics we never looked our parts:
"Can we have you holding up your hearts?"
We never had the attitude or look
We never made the film or wrote the book
We never got our music on the shelves
And only ever famous to ourselves,
We both became recluses, didn't care
We were not an ordinary pair.

Now, if you find crowsfeet round your eyes
Or some piffling ounces on your thighs
And the hint of puckering round your lips
God forbid – a pound upon your hips
Not to ever notice is my game

Telling you, you've always looked the same
Or ignoring everything you've said
Pleading urgent business in my shed
Since I'll only see the things I can
Am I not an ordinary man?

Should the winter ambush, with no warning
Let me set your grate up in the morning
Let me get your breakfast, make your coffee
Fetch bad-weather brandy from the offy
Be your Greyfriars Bobby who would wait
Even if the reaper made you late
Challenge him for you, and if I find him
Follow down the corridor behind him
Raging with the insults I would hurl
This was not an ordinary girl!

Time has dragged the sentiment from in me
Fear of losing you will underpin me
So in lieu of others in the past then
Let this be my Valentine at last then
Up the wooden hills again and gladly
Let them know we didn't do too badly
When we went from darkness into light
Ours was not an ordinary flight
You are not an ordinary dove
Ours is not an ordinary love.

EASTER BREAKS

The wolf of winter slinks away
Rheumy-eyed and creaky-jointed
Having risen, disappointed
Through the ragged woods she goes
Wrinkling her grizzled nose
Now the sun erects an awning
Steaming off the frosty morning
Laying his goods out on display
All the business of the day.

Easter wakes the dreaming suburbs
Calls to crescents in the spring
Now the lawns put on their bling
Daffodil and celandine
Dandelion and aconite
Cherry blossom stars the yards
The blackthorn snows them white.

Conscripted for a garden war
Recruit must now report to shed
Apprehensive, scratching head
Cursing unfamiliar mower
With its cutting-height much lower
Than can cope with Easter battles
It expires in clunks and rattles
Almost as if trying to say:
    "There is a green hill far away
    But I shall cut no grass today
    Not for you – nor Briggs&Stratton.
    Since the sun has got his hat on."

Within that gold-white Easter light
Across the fences, out of sight

A symphony of birdsong meets
In echoes of the greening streets
The hidden ball-games, clipping hedges
Laughter spilt from window ledges
Garage doors, a whistled tune
Which rises, falls, repeats and fades
All through the lime-green afternoon
The lime-green Easter afternoon.

THE LONG GAME

Not the handcuffs or the chains
Nor the tiny hourglass grains
Shifting imperceptibly
Time on time on time on time
But the telepathic link
After fading of the ink
With the sober overview
Following a heady climb.
Not the thee and not the thou
Nor the vow – that sacred cow
But the musing, looking back
Down the rosebay railway track
And the bet, the long-term bet
And the stifling of regret
And the trammel, shimmied through
Out of darkness, back to blue
Not the bringing to the boil
Or the drizzling of the oil
But the virtues and the faults
Sprinkled in like seasoning salts

Not the cradling of the head
Or recalling what was said
Nor the fragrance of the bed
But the workshop – and the shed
With the spanners and the wrench
Concentrating at the bench
On the nuts and bolts of life
These mechanics: Husband/wife.
Seamless, while their motives meet
One the rhythm, one the beat
One the wallet, one the purse
Each the earner, none the worse
After all the guests have gone
When the kettle-switch goes on
With the bottles put out back
And the dishes stacked in rack
Eve the tea, while Adam cleans
Only they know what that means
Only they know what that means…

A SUMMER DOWNPOUR

I battled with the bell-bine in the garden
Down on hands and knees in cauldron heat
By the raspberry canes and bright montbretia
The maths professor on his garden seat
Formulating calculations
Compound sums, abstruse equations.

Low on fuel, the bees were droning bombers
Pollen payload from the purple chives
Heavy in the humid air of summer

Limping sticky-engined back to hives
As the emperor sun took power
Lounging on St Mary's tower

Later on, the leaden sky grew darker
Round the front, the lime-tree leaves were waxy
Now the old professor found a problem
With a sigh, his spirit called a taxi
Penny-blots of summer rain
Wash his memory back again.

IN AUGUST

A drowzy, frowzy August
The sunrise is a gown
On the shoulders of the morning
When they hose the city down
In a scent of bread and flowers
The draymen drag the beer
Rolling kegs and barrels
On the see-saw of the year
Birdsongs disappear

Now they'll cram the airports
The yobs have gone abroad
A country tips its wages up
Sozzled as a lord
Late, the green tomatoes
Redden on the truss
And everyone's on holiday
Feet up on the bus
Everyone but us

Pulling up potato haulms
Tamping down the brazier
A bloom upon the damsons
And evenings getting hazier
Drifting through the gardens
In the damask of the day
August takes an encore
Stormclouds move away
For summer's last hooray
The afternoon's a guard dog
Dozing by the kennel
And everything is cider
Thistledown and fennel
Till autumn's in the jennel.

THIS IS WHAT SHE'S LIKE

She's the sunlight come
To prison cells
On frosty mornings
She's the last cigarette
Found in a forgotten raincoat
Late at night
She's a pale ghost
In a kimono
On a dusty landing
One Saturday morning
In summer when it rains
And tea is brewing downstairs
She treads on a splinter
And bleeds perfume
She's the sound of the key

In the latch at midnight
When you stop worrying
She's a kick in the shins
At a party and her handbag
Is a mystery
She's the dripping umbrella
In the kitchen
In February when the sun
Is forty watts anaemic
And taking iron tablets
She has a row of bottles
On the bathroom shelf
With strange white potions
Which smell of brilliant women
Who never got the credit
She's the telepathy between swans
Who fly upriver in pairs
Wings tipping the grey water
At dusk when summer is gone
And once a month
She's out on loan
To the moon
Careful with her.

BACK TO SCHOOL

Back to School, the words still loiter
On the corner of September
Presaging that sinking feeling
Many of us half-remember
During ebbing days of summer
Dragged out by a set-jawed mum

For the kitting-out and fitting
Which you knew would have to come
Stood in shops in too-large blazer
Wretched in your charcoal trews
Then to Freeman Hardy Willi*s*
For the dreaded *Vanguard* shoes
Two long limps behind the fashions
Durable and yet discreet
Glowering at you from the window
Little coffins for your feet
Back to school, the smell of apples
Paper, pencil-cases, Jeyes
Low-slung sunlight, raking blackboards
Calibrating shorter days
Later, when the dust had settled
Autumn term got into gear
Horses fell in step, the wagon
Rumbled down the dying year.

REMEMBRANCE

For homefires, lions and roses
When the sky was overcast
And the sinew left of England
Turned its back upon the past
And the guns fell quiet at last

For one bird singing sweetly
From fields far beyond
When winter coughed discreetly
In the forest of Rethondes
And black rain swelled the pond

For horseflesh, lead and leather
And the broken-shafted cart
For friends who fell together
And the farmer losing heart
When ploughing couldn't start

For the spectral rails stretching
To the future's gaping yawn
A patient's shaky sketching
And a family left forlorn
– For talent never born

For sterling girls and mothers
On clifflands seen from France
For promises to others
When ordered to advance
For the lack of song and dance

For hamlet, town and village
Where lads came back alone
War's ullage and war's spillage
In native blood and bone
Immortalised in stone.

BONFIRE NIGHT

Branches dragged from scrubby woods
By rough and holey-jumpered lads
Bits and bats from mildewed sheds
Surrendered by their dads
On grey old days, the pallid sun
Got up and shook his head.

Had a look – thought better of it
Then went back to bed.
In dripping trees on misty recs
A smell of coal and weekday stew
Went drifting on the chestnut days
All the while the bonfire grew
A requisitioning of clothes
For a lumpy, lolling Guy
Grinning on a broken chair
Straw and paper everywhere

'Genies' hung in windless ginnels
Where the lads had lit the powder
From a broken penny banger
– Aerial Bombs were louder
Pram-wheels creaking under carties
Hauling paper, leaves and kindling
After clocks went back for winter
With the daylight hours dwindling
Silhouettes emerged from porches
Torches, muted conversations
Rocket from a muddy bottle
Opening the celebrations
Cracking flames went licking up
Their orange gobbets in the night
Ancient sorrows of a summer
Guy and bonfire all alight.

OUR NEW LOVE, THE BUS

Let's take the 78 in early winter
When all the oaks are turning gold
From Tenpenny Hill to Thorrington
In mid-November sunlight after rain
And kiss outside the Co-op here
Till 4.16... and then 4.36...

THEN AT THESE MINUTES
    PAST EACH HOUR

Until all the buses stop running
A full hour short of closing-time
From now on sweetheart, it is only you
The driver and that gum-chewing girl
Who meets her mates at Brightlingsea,
A shivering, knackered office cleaner
An old bloke back from seeing a son in jail
And some kid talking draw-deals on a phone
For these will be our fellow travellers
The very young, the aged and the car-less

And out along the estuary at tea-time
The headlamps dash the fields and lanes
And rake the stops where no-one waits
Who ever graduated to a car

DO NOT STAND FORWARD
    OF THIS POINT

Past a pub, a sign, a level-crossing
The new estate lit up like Lucozade
Deserted, but for hooded boys on bikes
A bell, a groan of brakes, a hiss of doors

Then back onto the rabbit-splattered road
The rattling draughty taxi's now our own

So let us take this 78 in winter
While all the world is busy driving home
One to each car and cursing at the traffic
Because apart from us and all these ghosts

34 SEATED AND NINE STANDING

We may well find, at last, that we're alone.

WINTER WOODSMOKE

Suspended in the winter chill
Of Christmas Eve, upon the hill
A smoke hung on the red-rimmed sun
The bonfire was begun
By someone not too far away
Some good old boy, stepped out that day
Who fancied he might have a fire
Build the year a funeral pyre
– Steal an hour or two to think
Before a Christmas drink.

The winter blossomed in that blaze
The dwindling of December days
In holly berries brighter then
Than anyone remembered when
Who knew the wooded hills and lanes
– Recalling frosted window panes
The glacier-minted morning light

In cottage bedrooms after night
Under a childhood eiderdown
Or stood in rough old dressing gown
Inherited from older teens.
Now, struggling into jumpers, jeans
Palmolive soap and tea downstairs
The collies by the kitchen chairs
Nosing round the a la carte
Prior to a seasonal start
Soliciting for morsels left
And risking sundry kicks for theft.
The morning sun, its low-slung rays
Splintered through the fuggy haze
Of kitchen steam – the pilot lit
The boiler grumbling over it
A frying-pan, lightly smoking there
And Christmas spirit in the air:
"Now, chop the kindling, fetch some logs
And walk those dogs!"

The smoke fanned out, a lazy blue
Across the fleece of oaks, and through
The last gold ingots on the birch
Beside a greystone church
A lone old woman, in that place
Arranging flowers, her pensive face
Remembering the wartime planes
Autumn fields like counterpanes
Widowhood and paper chains
Lychgates – winter rains.

And in the Old Town, down below
At Christmas, all those years ago
The gladrag restaurants and hotels

Rich in port-and-pudding smells
The lunchtime clatter and the roar
Which issued from the kitchen door
The chefs and front-of-house at war
From starter, through to *petits fours.*
The rich old ducks and tweedy toffs
Glugging tinctures for their coughs
As waiters minnied round with gin
And porters dragged potatoes in
A clerk while working out a bill
Observed the blaze upon the hill
And noted how the skeins of grey
Like chiffon scarves, draped on the day.
Came drifting, rather gently down
All afternoon towards the town
To hang by railway bridges there
Squatting on the frosty air;
A fragrance made of leaves and bark
As sweet in that encroaching dark
Which covered up the guttering sun,
As chestnuts, slightly overdone,
Peeled on littered front-room floors
When all the lights go on indoors

And in that moment, nothing's said
The birds will put themselves to bed
And silence reigning in the hedge
Will reach the woodland edge
And from the dying fire, the crown
A shower of sparks, its seeing-down.
A ballet for the winter night.
Out of darkness into light
The dwindling of December days
Which blossom in that blaze.

THE DARK DAYS DOWN TO CHRISTMAS

The dark days down to Christmas paw
Like horses at an earthen floor
When all the ghosts of autumn pass away
And ragged squads of starlings fight
In firethorn trees in fading light
For orange berries brighter than the day

The dark days down to Christmas slip
As convicts from a prison ship
Down moonlit ropes and hawsers one by one
And past the quayside through the lanes
With winter dragging on their chains
Peer into windows, envious of the sun

The dark days down to Christmas creep
As wolves around a pen of sheep
When people turn their collars up and sigh
A convalescent crescent moon
Comes drifting out mid-afternoon
To bid an old arthritic year goodbye

And down the drain these dark days spin
As kindling wood and paraffin
And sacks of coal and logs are fed
Into a spider-haunted shed
The garden tools with cobweb tines
And skeins of string on withered vines
Are vestiges left hanging on
As evidence of summer gone

The dark days down to Christmas call
In echoes to a flagstoned hall
Too early for the feast, they stay awhile
But each, an uninvited guest
Is dirty, cold and under-dressed
And slips away unmissed in single file

The dark days down to Christmas wait
Like cinders cricking in a grate
Before the fire is raked, re-set and lit
And cheerless in their unmade bed
Glow only very faintly red
But give no hint of heat in spite of it

And yet with each dark day complete
Lighter and brighter grows the street
As frantic in the pubs and shops
The work speeds up – for soon, it stops
And in a lull between the two
The last day, having much to do
Though up till now, no time for thought
Allows a warming glass of port

And having set an hour free
Before the lights go on for tea
As ingots of old sunlight pierce the gloom
A ghost parade of days appears
With paler days from other years
Who reminisce in whispers round the room

The last day down to Christmas ends
Excusing all his sullen friends
Who slave until December twenty-third
Cut mistletoe, deliver parcels

Light the cottages like castles
Scribble cards and hardly say a word
Then, having done their tasks they drift
As workers from a graveyard shift
The moment that each day has lost its light
Till wistfully, the last one goes
Ignites a candle, leaves a rose
And slips out softly to the frosty night.

THE SONG OF
THE WATERLILY

Chorus

From keel and keelson,
strakes and sails

From floors and decking
up to mast

We'll pull together stem to stern
We are the ship, a ship at last.

We'll pull together, pull together
Any weather sky can cast

Pull together, stem to stern
We are the ship, a ship at last.

The Song of the Parts

A wooden boat, un-named, untried
Lies moored and waiting for the tide
With maiden voyage due next day
A light wind ushers night away.
As if to praise the shipwright's arts
A hubbub rises from her parts
As one by one, each sings its song
To prove the previous singer wrong:

"I am The Keel, therefore the king
For me, the adze and whetstone sing
To shape me, scarve me for my reign
Along the length of my demesne

I am the strength, I am the spine
The spirit of the ship is mine
And hewn from woodland oak so tall
Take precedence above you all."

"I am The Stem, I rule the bow
The Keel will kneel before me now
And once I'm hoisted into place
Let no-one claim a stronger case
Apart perhaps, from just one other
Since I have a distant brother
In The Sternpost whom you'll see
Located to the aft of me.

Stem and Sternpost, stern and stem
The Keel depends on both of them
Between us both, the reign is halved
The Stern is tenoned, Stem is scarved
But nonetheless these dual kings
Shall rule above all other things
And every lowly plank and wale
Shall pay us tribute when we sail."

"We are The Deadwoods, timber blocks
Who help insure against such shocks
The previous kings may not withstand
Despite pretensions of being grand
And while they are affixed to us
They have no right to boast, discuss
Their sovereignty above the rest
Until their strength is put to test."

"We are The Floors – of old, The Flowers
Those timbers which retain the powers

To be the proving of this boat
And all who sail her, once afloat.
So here across the keel we lie
The shipwright's hammer standing by
Must clench us, Keel and Keelson, in
Before all other jobs begin."

"I am The Keelson, king-to-be
The Keel is weak, deprived of me
I'm like my father, made of joints
And scarved – although at different points
I am the power behind his throne
He'd break, were he to reign alone
If not for all this work I do
So though I'm hidden, I reign too."

"We are The Futtocks, ribs are we
To brace the planking 'gainst the sea
From ancient oak, its branches chained,
We're cut to shape. The strakes constrained
By our full strength, provide the shield
From any blow the storm may wield
While laying siege to breech the wood
Without our help, the boat's no good."

"We are The Planks, The Strakes and Wales
No ship that sailed – or ever sails
Can do so till we're fitted in
To help provide her with her skin
The sheer-strake first and then the rest
Once plied to shape in steaming chest
Are lifted, fitted, spiked in place
To give the finished craft its grace."

"We are The Deckbeams, in a storm
We help preserve the vessel's form
We're laid athwartships, once we're down
The Decking then shall be our gown
For men to work and walk upon
The cygnet now becomes a swan.
Without us at the vessel's hub
The ship would merely be a tub."

"I am The Oakum, humble stuff
From hemp or jute, a greasy fluff
Of fibres, forced into the gaps
Between the planks, by mallet taps
I'm sealed with pitch until just right
To make the vessel watertight
The boat's no use to anyone
If caulkyer's work is left undone."

"We are The Sails and The Mast
And though we may be fitted last
We catch all winds to make our slaves
And push the boat across the waves
The master Mast, holds Sail, the dame
With chest puffed out, she'll justly claim
Without her ballet in the air
The boat will languish, drifting there."

"All very well!" The Tiller creaks
The Rudder cricking, as he speaks:
"A pretty pas-de-deux my dear.
Yet pointless, if you cannot steer
The wind's your master not your slave
And can't be trusted to behave

Since once the vessel is afloat,
It's we two parts control this boat."

And now the parts had had their say
Unproved and quiet the new ship lay
While carpenters and riggers came
Her owners pondered on a name
With maiden voyage looming up
They drink a toast. Her christening cup
Is drained until the liquor's gone
And Waterlily settled on.

Rock'n'Roll

A NEW BLUE MOON –
The Birth Of British Rock 1955-1960

A decade after World War Two
A melancholy nation,
Awaking like a patient
From a dodgy operation
In tenements and back-to-backs
In blackened towns with cindertracks
By bombsite rosebay willowherb
On hopscotch chalkmark, dog-muck kerb
The smells of cabbage, malting grain
And coal-smoke wafting on the rain
A people, haunted by their past
That beckoned endless, ancient, vast
Would best-foot forward, as before
March down history's corridor
The half-pint urchins, childhood gone
– Eclipsed by war – were quietly glad
To put their first long trousers on
Each boy a copy of his dad
Each girl a model of her mum
Expecting nothing more than that
With adulthood and peace now come.

By autumn '55, the charts
Gave scarcely any clue at all.
The summer saw a clothing craze
For USA-style jeans, it's true
But nothing in the smoggy air
Had indicated change was due
The 'hit parade' a few months old
Its titles on a pegboard wall
Read Frankie Laine and Johnny Ray

Winnie Atwell, Doris Day
Everything seemed safe and sound
And twenty shillings in the pound

One o'clock, two o'clock, three o'clock rock

Avuncular, at thirty-odd
A kiss-curl, honest farmhand face
Bill Haley and his Comets came
To launch the rocket into space

Ten o'clock, eleven o'clock twelve o'clock rock

A country full of boys and girls
All acned, awkward and repressed
Came jiving out, one autumn night
Unrefined and under-dressed

We're gonna rock

And now the dancehalls caught alight
In northern city, seaside town
The councillors would curse this blight
An edifice of years torn down

Around the clock

The national servicemen returned
From Nicosia, Berlin, Benghazi
To dark, bronchitic, terraced rows
The pigeon-loft, an outside khazi

Tonight!

The winter trees in pea-soup fog
A country yearning for its spring
And George the old king, three years dead
With skiffle whistling in the wings
Along came Elvis – King of Kings.

A poor young southern trucker
Grown hungry with the blues
He'd gone to visit Scotty Moore
In pink suit and white shoes:
"If I could find a white man
Who had that Negro sound"
Sam Phillips said:
"I'd make a billion dollars…"
Presley crowned.
A jukebox was delivered
The records now arrived
The King was in gold lamé
The world stood up and jived.

Take your dad-rags off and try
The brothel-creepers, bootlace tie
The drape, the drainies and the quiff
For Elvis, Tommy, Gene and Cliff
The jukebox flashed,
The stars came out
The critics glumly stood about
Apprehensive and askance
While Frankenstein began to dance.

The Papers (not the media yet)
Would fulminate against this fad
The preacher in his pulpit fumed
While apoplectic mum and dad

Must go to war on errant son
New café culture had begun:
In Soho – in Edwardian garb
To the *2 I's* or *Le Macabre*
Our embryonic rockers went
Sought refuge from parental storms
Back home in Middlesex or Kent
The peace was broken, rules were bent
In suburbs where the beat craze sent
Its rhizomes spreading underground
As boys sprang up who'd make the sound.
The skiffle strummed in coffee bars
Would sell a thousand cheap guitars
To folkies, bluesers and the rest
Who bleeding-fingered, did their best
With cheesewire fretboards, out-of-tune
To learn *Tom Dooley* or *Blue Moon*.

And now the groups began to tour
With red guitars, the glittering drums
A champagne-sparkle on their sides
The splashes, sizzles and the rides
The little clothbound amps – a case
Of over-driven valves – the bass,
The heavy upright stands, the boom.
That noise that shook each function room
Became the throbbing heart – the soul
Of early British rock and roll.

The US stars flew in to play
The Corn Exchanges, Saturday
In towns whose names were only said
When weekly football scores were read:
Little Richard, coming *here*?

To Yorkshire pud and Watneys beer?
Buddy, Chuck and Jerry Lee
Waking up to Brooke Bond Tea?
Every legend on the road
And only Presley never showed.
Lonely Presley never showed
Where rock'n'roll would bare its teeth
In Swindon, Huddersfield or Neath
The combo was the finest choice
Since Mr Rolls met Mr Royce.

Though now the businessmen moved in
The shiny suit, the phone, the fin
Came following the jangly noise
The smell of money, witless boys
Pretty, packaged, heaven-sent
Mister Twenty-five Percent
Would have the know-how and the nous
The penthouse pad, or country house
The aftershave and signet rings
He knew so much about these things
And might protect our guile-less kid
From shysters with a lesser bid
The boys were taken on and groomed,
The tracts on etiquette consumed
And given names with girl-appeal
Like Wilde, Power, Faith or Steele
Made fodder for the pin-up page
On pushed out on the West End stage
As showbiz tried to take control
Of early British rock and roll

The music, like a strain of flu
Now spread its symptoms all around
Via *Luxembourg* – which had to do
For swishing torchlit radio sound

Via handsome gypsy fairground boys
Squat jackets checked like marzipan
The joyful, whip and dodgem noise
Our crusty elders tried to ban.
Via television taking wing
With *6.5 Special* and *Oh Boy*
The sound headmasters hated
Curated by the hoi-polloi

An England ruled by silver spoon
Its pubs that closed all afternoon
Its labourers who'd learnt to croon
Ga-ding a-dong a-ding Blue Moon
Its midwives cycling side-by-side
Its men who pottered in their sheds
Threw up their hands at once and cried:
"We'll all be murdered in our beds!"
And yet from church-run, youth-club huts
There came no mayhem – nowhere near
Not even when a voice piped-up:
"Hey! Why not do the show right here?"
And so the British beat was born
And *then* the Sixties start to dawn

Though looking back along the tracks
A scant five years has passed so far
Since Haley, drummer, keyboard, sax
Accordian, bass and lead guitar

Flew in flew out, prepared the ground
A place to land the UFO
The sound that turned the world around
By some young guy from Tupelo

In Geordieland and Liverpool
In London, Edinburgh and Leeds
In rooms above the papershops
In backstreet pubs they sow the seeds
That twang which cuts the starry night
The slapback echo in the air
Will change the world from black and white
The fights will happen over hair
And hems of skirts and pointy shoes
When elders start a war with kids
Which time dictates that they will lose

In England ruled by silver spoon
With pubs which close all afternoon
The milkmen whistle some old tune:
Bom baba bom
Ba-bom ba-bom bom
Baba Bom ba-ba-bom
Ga-dang ga-dang dang
Ga-dinga donga ding…
                    Blue
                        Moooon

I Hank Marvinned

I Hank Marvinned
We all did
With cricket bats
In front of a mirror
In our bedrooms
After school
I Hank Marvinned
Quite regularly
My mother nearly caught me
What were you doing
Nothing mum
Cricket bat still warm
I Hank Marvinned
Unashamedly
On the bed sometimes
Standing up
I knew all the dance steps
I thought I'd grow out of it
When I got married
But the other day
When she was out
I Hank Marvinned
In the living room
I straightened the place out
Afterwards
But somehow she found out
I'd been seen
You Hank Marvinned?
At your age?
She made me burn my cricket bat
And see a psychiatrist
I go to a special group now

Once a week
They give us all cricket bats
And black-framed spectacles
And we have to do it
Hank Marvin
In front of everybody
It's pathetic
Half a dozen men
In their late forties
Cricket bats in hands
Spectacles on
Doing the dance steps
Grinning inanely
Shadows
Of our former selves.

RINGO STARR

Ringo Starr, Ringo Starr
Nodding-dog in Beatles car
Dingle drummer, Ludwig kit
Kept the beat and sang a bit

Ringo Starr, Ringo Starr
Mad to let him near guitar
Master of the tom-tom roll
Narrowly escaped the dole

Ringo Starr, Ringo Starr
Clinking cowbells, four each bar
Teenage memories coming back
Oh no. It's the Ringo track.

Ringo Starr, Ringo Starr
Better than Dave Clark by far
Never seemed to be as 'gear'
Once he had his own career

Ringo Starr, Ringo Starr
Did the drums on Drive My Car
Took a glammy second wife
Having had a hard day's life.

LATIN DOLL

One evening in Ibiza
The dancers took a breather
As Hildegard von Bingen
Went ambient in the ether

A raver stood there startled
The atmosphere seemed odd:
"Whar kind of House is *this* then?"
A nun barked: "House of God."

For centuries, essential
At Evensong or Matin
She chilled a lot of churches
And crucially, in Latin

Young man, man you ought to try it
The liquor, herbs and sound
Till you've been Benedictined
You haven't been around."

Did Hildegard know singin'?
Does cows milk come in pints?
Go ask the nuns of Bingen
It's ten miles west of Mainz.

JOHN COOPER CLARKE

John Cooper Clarke
Lives in the dark
And won't emerge
Till well gone three
Unlike Attila
Unlike me
His accent
Indicates the north
He leaves it late
To sally forth
With pointy boots
And skinny suits

Vacates his lair
With back-combed hair
A plastic bag
And purloined fag
His aching dental cavity
The wages of depravity

John Cooper Clarke
Nocturnal, stark
You'll never meet him
In the park

But if you really
Wish to see him
Try a stylish mausoleum.

TEN REASON WHY HE'S DAVID BOWIE ... AND YOU'RE NOT

David uses *his* spare time
For dreaming up new styles
He never spends Whit Monday
In the bathroom, grouting tiles

David's early efforts
Often dwelt on alienation
He never noted diesels
Or hung out on Reading Station

David shaved both eyebrows
And the net effect was 'arty'
He never had just one done
While unconscious at a party

David in his sixth decade
Still has a head of hair on
And not some strands resembling
A bar-code printed thereon

David orders goodies
From an oriental tea-shop
He doesn't trawl for bargains
In the Pound & Fifty Pee Shop

David dabbled earlier on
In Genet, Brecht, Fassbinder
He didn't lie on sofas
Drinking 'Spesh' and watching *Minder*

David put on make-up
And a dress, in search of glamour
And unlike you, he wasn't chased
By skinheads with a hammer

David says: "Good evening
Here's a song of mine from *Low*."
And never: "Aw-right, Dog's Head?
This is one by Status Quo."

Another thing with David
He keeps himself in trim
But the single biggest difference is
Your wife still fancies *him*.

AN A TO Z OF THE RECORDING STUDIO

A's for assistant, or 'tape-op' to me
An attitude problem, employed to make tea
B is for brass-players, grumpily sat
Cursing the song, when it's not in B flat

C's for computers and current conditions
Helping the world Do away with musicians
E is for engineer, flakey as hell
Handsomely paid, so he hides it quite well

F is for 'fade out' a popular trend
Saves the musicians rehearsing an end
G's for guitarist whose solo's too long
And 'groove' an excuse for not writing the song.

H is for harp-players, blowing too hot
I is for interface, which they do not.
J's for Japan, where they make all the gear
And where it returns, if it can't be fixed here.

K is keyboard, essential of course
Its manual is printed in runic Old Norse
L is for limiter, looping and licks
Or lead-guitar solo, you lose in the mix.

M is for monitors, written as *MON*
And N for the notes we repair later on
O can be 'out-take' or sometimes 'outboard'
But often: "Oh bugger. It didn't record."

P is for programmer, also for Pod
The second's a gizmo, the first thinks he's God
Q is for Q-tips for head-cleaning jobs
Removing the grunge under pan-pots and knobs

R is for reverb in rack on the shelf
Which helps a bad vocalist live with himself
S is for sibilance which we don't need
T is for Top, causing earholes to bleed

U is for 'usable' often the one
Backing track used, if it can't be undone
V is for volume, which we know as 'Gain'
And 'very close' which means: 'Do it again'

W's "Why can't I hear what I've played?"
Exes are all that the backing band's paid.
Y is for Yamaha NS10s (*Yawn*)
And Z is for Zizz, when you crawl out at dawn.

THE DEATH OF JOHN ENTWISTLE

In Bach baroque, his bass-line boom
That looms so large, will still leave room
For Townshend's whirling windmill tune
The snares and cymbals of Keith Moon
And whilst this mayhem's going on
He never bats an eyelid, John.

Amidst a howling feedback sound
With Moonie's tom-toms rolling round
The smoke, the damage and the fights.
The twirling mics and flashing lights
All common sense packed up and gone
Stock-still stands John and carries on.

That's him, the bassist's bass-player there
The wannabes wil come to stare
Yet come unstuck when it seems clear
He plays it faster than they hear
And louder. Louder – phon for phon
Than all the other players, John.

The tape's unlaced, the playback head
Won't play the song, the amps are dead
The tape tails-out, but all this pop
This racket that we made, won't stop

Those notes un-struck upon the staves
We take them with us to our graves.

They'll miss him all those blue-eyed boys
Who grew up with that Sixties noise
Commiserate in beers, then sigh
And wonder how the years got by
With Keith? A given. Never John.
And that's the rhythm section gone.

The quiet man in the market place
Played other things apart from bass
He didn't advertise as such
He wasn't interviewed, that much.
When all the other stuff went on.
He blew his trumpet quietly, John.

THE SPIRIT OF SYD BARRETT

Like an orange tree in winter
With summer gone too soon
In a spray of fallen blossom
From a sunny afternoon
To the dark side of the moon

From golden Cambridge gardens
Where the pop star threw his toys
To the midnight courts of London
And the psychedelic noise
Of chiming English boys

But when the trip was over
And after overload
Poor Syd came cycling softly
Up the Cherry Hinton road
Ignoring sundry students
The fans who called for more
The French and German journalists
Who hung around his door.
He told them, "Syd's not here now."
He cannot talk today
His pigeons are not homing
He can't come out to play.

Recluse, so rich in whimsy
Still played and still discussed
A madcap loved long after
His scarecrow turned to dust
And bike began to rust.

Barefoot, the summer stolen
In strains of songs unborn
The spirit of Syd Barrett
Goes home across the lawn
Towards the gates of dawn.

Backwords

A few of these poems go back almost twenty years, to the late 1980s. Before that I'd been a musician and a songwriter whose fortunes had varied somewhat. Writing, which I'd done since I was a child, had always been a sort of secret retreat for me. I began writing for music fanzines in my twenties and once, in 1984, I got a break with a big piece in *The Guardian* about the Miners Strike. In early 1988, after an illness and finding myself temporarily of no fixed abode, I entered a regional poetry competition to try and win some money. I was down to my last few pounds and considering having to sell my piano. To my surprise I won the competition, found more work and the piano was saved. I came out of the closet as a poet and in almost a reverse image of my fortunes in the music business, within about a year, I had found success. I became a regular pop poet with *The Independent* newspaper – a working relationship which would continue for fifteen years. During that time, I often wrote anything up to three poems a week for them. The editor Simon Kelner and his then-deputy Tristan Davies pushed me to feats that would have been beyond my capabilities in earlier days. I would for instance, be asked to write a front page poem, at a few hours notice. I would sometimes be commissioned for a piece of satirical verse to fill a page, at a day's notice. I became an unstable alloy of journalist and poet.

At the same time, I began doing small jobs for BBC Radio and getting a bit of local TV work, in addition to taking subject-related commissions from other sources. All of this time, still driven by the fear of a return to the poverty I'd known, I took all the live work that fate threw at me. In 1997 for instance, I did a poetry tour of some twenty five gigs over thirty-one days, during which time, I wrote my pieces for the paper on trains and in hotel rooms. When I left the *Independent on Sunday*, I became poet at *The Sunday Express*, for whom I'd written occasional features and whose editor Martin Townsend now pushes me to similarly high standards of work. He sent me to The Falkland Isles in 2007 and I filed my copy from there. Once, when I asked him if I could re-write something I'd already sent, because I felt that it wasn't up to scratch, he laughed and described my pursuit of poetry as 'Arthurian'. But I try to treat every job as if it were my last and I never let up – in case it is.

If I have been successful, I think it is because my poems rhyme, are mostly humorous and are delivered quickly and to order. When I began, I thought that since I was now a working poet it was an incredible stroke of good luck I'd had and that I ought to work at it as hard as I could. Years in rock bands writing lyrics for my own songs and those of my fellow musicians, most notably my friend Captain Sensible – a perfectionist – had made me very tough-minded and given me immense stamina.

This collection is the best of my work. It was amazing going back through it all. Files and files of the stuff as well as a dozen of my previously-published books. The earlier poems were typed on an old thirty-quid Bulgarian typewriter. Then I upgraded to a heavy, reconditioned Olympia manual typewriter. Then an electric. Then two word processors. Then a laptop. I'm now on my third laptop.

I don't know any literary bodies, don't usually get asked to any special events and I don't go in for competitions, bursaries or prizes. I haven't had the time really and anyway, I don't think that my sort of poetry is the kind of stuff that they're looking for. I don't regard myself as having a career. I just work. I love it. I don't think of myself as being a heavyweight poet – not by any modern definitions anyway – but as more of a kind of rhyming cartoonist, maybe mining the same kind of seam as William Hogarth or Carl Giles. I'm definitely more country than town and though I love London a good deal, I don't really hang out there for very long. I have my haunts but they aren't anywhere where the movers and shakers go.

In this collection are poems about Essex and East Anglia where I live and which I love. There are also poems about rock stars and rock culture which were my roots and also my route into the wider arts world. There are satires and pastiches and all sorts of dreadful puns and there's probably quite a bit of nostalgia. Of the unusual words here, there are only a few that may need explaining: a *seax* or *sceacs* was the name of the Saxon sword, three of which adorn the Essex coat of arms, a *ginnel* or *jennel* is the little narrow alleyway found in between rows of terraced houses, *twoc* or *twoccing* means taking a car without the owner's consent, and there's also probably a bit of recording studio jargon in here too. There certainly isn't enough to justify a glossary however. This collection is meant to be dipped into, rifled through and generally left lying around for casual snacking. That's what it's there for. Do please, use it.

Martin Newell